Quicl

QUICK ESCAPES® FROM
Seattle

· · · · · · · · · · · · · · · · · · · ·

The Best Weekend Getaways

FIRST EDITION

Christine A. Cunningham

gPP®
travel
Guilford, Connecticut

All the information in this guidebook is subject to change.
We recommend that you call ahead to obtain
current information before traveling.

Quick Escapes is a registered trademark of Globe Pequot Press.

Editor: Kevin Sirois
Project Editor: Meredith Dias
Layout: Sue Murray
Text design: Sheryl Kober
Maps: Ryan Mitchell © Morris Book Publishing, LLC.

Library of Congress Cataloging-in-Publication Data is available on file.

ISBN 978-0-7627-5450-2

Printed in the United States of America
10 9 8 7 6 5 4 3 2 1

CONTENTS

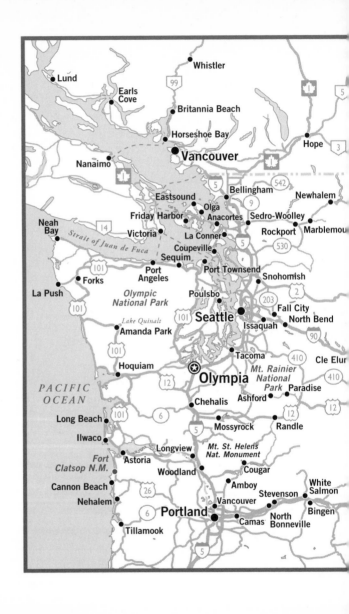

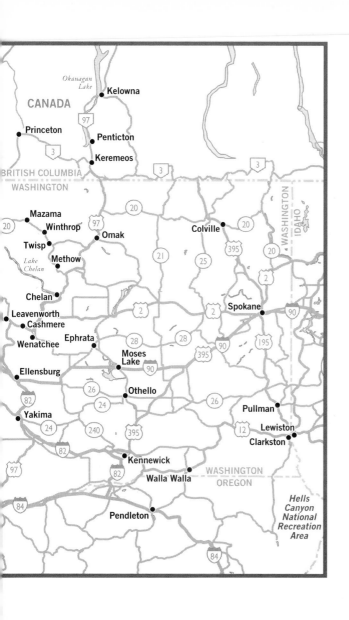

ABOUT THE AUTHOR

Christine A. Cunningham is a freelance writer and editor who lives in Eugene, Oregon, with her husband, Pete Peterson. The remarkably diverse Northwest landscape intrigues her as much now as it did when she settled there from the San Francisco Bay Area almost 40 years ago. She publishes mainly in health and business magazines but has written a number of food, outdoor, and travel articles for regional newspapers and magazines. She is the author of *Quick Escapes from Portland, OR,* and revised and updated five editions of *Quick Escapes Pacific Northwest* and the second edition of *Fun with the Family Oregon.*

INTRODUCTION

This guide to brief getaways from Seattle is intended for longtime residents, newcomers to the Pacific Northwest, and visitors passing through—anyone who's eager to explore the recreational wonderland that lies beyond the major cities of the region.

When you want to travel scenic byways and discover their hidden treasures, take this book with you. It will lead you to well-known spots that no tourist should miss and will uncover hideaways that only the local folk know.

The guide provides fully detailed itineraries, much like a customized, organized tour. But they are suggestions only! Don't try to do everything listed on each trip, or you'll feel too rushed to enjoy yourself. Pick and choose among the activities, and plan to return for those you missed.

At the end of each chapter, the **There's More** section provides additional reasons to come back. **Special Events** lists regional events and holiday activities. **Other Recommended Restaurants and Lodging** gives concise descriptions of good places to eat and stay other than those included in the itinerary. Finally, **For More Information** tells you whom to contact to obtain maps and learn about the area you're visiting.

The itineraries are designed as auto tours, but public transport, walking, and bicycling are viable alternatives in many cases. I recommend using them whenever you can.

Consider traveling in the off-season, rather than the high-use summer months. The weather is mild in spring and fall, though rains are frequent in the spring. Winter has its own appeal, with the crowds gone and the landscape spare or clad in white. Be advised, however, that some roads are closed in the winter, such as Southbound Escapes to Mount Rainier (SR 410/123) and Mount St. Helens (FR 99).

Wheelchair-accessible facilities are mentioned where appropriate.

Rates and fees are not specifically stated, as they often change, but you may assume that most costs are reasonable. If a place seems unusually expensive (or amazingly inexpensive), I have so indicated. Museums usually charge a nominal admission fee or request a donation. I have indicated when they are free.

Distances are approximate and are expressed in miles. American standard spelling is used throughout.

Make reservations in advance at hotels, bed-and-breakfasts, and inns whenever possible. Some are very small, and rooms fill up quickly, especially from May through October.

The following is a list of standard equipment you'll probably need or find useful on your escapes:

- Rain gear (In the Northwest, the weather is unpredictable.)
- Travel-size umbrella
- Warm jacket
- Sturdy walking shoes and wading shoes
- Day pack
- Water bottle
- Insect repellent
- Camera, with extra batteries and memory
- Cell phone
- Compass or GPS
- Regional maps
- Binoculars
- Flashlight
- First-aid kit
- Blankets
- Pocket knife with corkscrew
- Cooler and ice packs for picnic lunches

EMERGENCY NUMBERS

- **State Police:** 911
- **Roadside Assistance & Emergencies:** 911 (statewide)
- **Washington State Ferries:** (888) 808-7977 or (206) 464-6400
- **Road Conditions and Road Closure Information:** 511 or visit WSDOT's traveler website at www.wsdot.wa.gov/traffic

NORTHBOUND *ESCAPES*

NORTHBOUND ESCAPE *One*

Skagit County
WANDERING THROUGH SPRING GARDENS / 1 NIGHT

Antiques shops
Fields of spring flowers
Fine art galleries
Picturesque waterfront
Northwest art museum
Wildlife refuge

Here's a 2-day sojourn in the country, a brief escape that bursts with the vibrant colors of tulip and daffodil fields, and is home to several well-designed nurseries and demonstration gardens, including Christianson's Nursery, RoozenGaarde, Skagit Valley Gardens, and the Washington State University Volunteer Display Gardens. This escape allows time to stroll through several gardens, before continuing to La Conner, just 8 miles away. In La Conner, serious shoppers can browse to their hearts' content in this delta-side artists' colony, with its host of shops and galleries holding unexpected treasures. The small town's thriving downtown area is packed with tourists on summer weekends and during the tulip festival, but even then, visitors who venture along the quiet back roads can observe wildlife, smell flowers, and revel in rural serenity.

DAY 1 / MORNING

Drive north on I-5 to Mount Vernon before crossing the Skagit River to SR 20 (about 60 miles). Visit the **Skagit Valley Gardens,** 18923 Peter Johnson Rd. (360-424-6760 or 800-732-3266; www.skagit valleygardens.com), one of the oldest public display gardens in Skagit County. This year-round botanical garden displays thousands of tulips, crocuses, and daffodils in the spring; brilliant annuals in

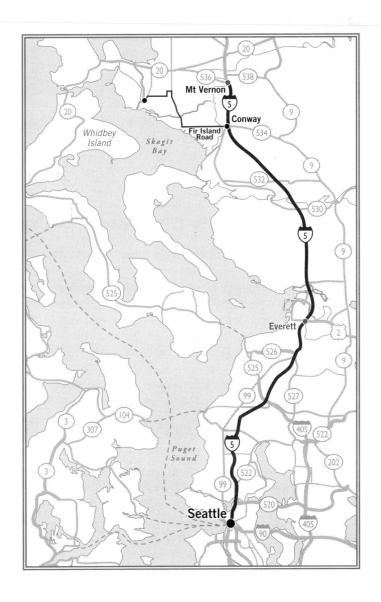

August; and festive poinsettias in December. Visitors are welcome to have picnic lunches in the nursery gazebo. Also in Mount Vernon is **RoozenGaarde,** 15867 Beaver Marsh Rd. (360-424-8531; www .tulips.com), where you will find a 3-acre display garden and gift shop. It's open Monday through Saturday 9 a.m. to 6 p.m., and Sunday 11 a.m. to 4 p.m. You're in for a visual feast if your visit coincides with the nursery's main blooming season, which is late February to late July.

Be sure to visit the **Padilla Bay National Estuarine Research Reserve,** 10441 Bayview-Edison Rd., Mt. Vernon (360-428-1558; www.padillabay.gov), which offers hands-on learning about the adjacent estuary. Bayview-Edison Road edges the shore of Padilla Bay, a body of water well protected by a group of islands: Fidalgo, Guemes, and Samish. The reserve is one in a nationwide system that teaches visitors about estuaries—mixes of salt water and fresh-water. Walk the uplands nature trail, view aquatic displays and Padilla Bay, and if you're still curious, learn more in the center's research library. Hours vary seasonally.

Retrace your steps and cross SR 20. You are now on Best Road, in the heart of the tulip, iris, and daffodil fields of the Skagit Valley, where great swaths of springtime color draw hordes of admirers. The fertile farmlands of Skagit Valley are among the world's top growers of tulips.

In other seasons the valley is equally beautiful, if not as brightly colored, with tawny fields undulating in summer breezes and autumn mists drifting through flame-hued maples. Mount Baker stands on the far horizon, a towering, snow-mantled cone.

When you come to **La Conner Flats Rhododendron Garden,** 15920 Best Rd. (360-466-3190), stop for a tour of an authentic 230-acre English country garden. Eleven acres bloom with color, from March's daffodils and rhododendrons to June's roses, August's dahlias, and October's crimson foliage. In addition to the array of flowers are gardens brimming with herbs, vegetables, and berries.

AFTERNOON

Continue on Best Road to Chilberg Road, and turn west toward **La Conner** proper. The historic, picturesque little town had its beginnings in 1867 as a trading post. A few years later, John Conner, from Olympia, bought the store and town, as well as 70 additional acres, for the sum of $500. In 1872 he named the settlement after his wife, Louisa Ann Conner, using just her initials.

La Conner, perched on the edge of Swinomish Channel, which lies between the mainland and Fidalgo Island, grew into an active port and fishing community. But when the Great Depression brought those industries to a standstill, La Conner began to fade.

In the 1970s, energetic townsfolk decided to make some changes to encourage tourism. They have taken great pains to maintain the locale's history through architectural preservation, and now more than 160 buildings are listed on the National Register of Historic Places. The city council remains steadfast about maintaining similar architectural facades and subtle earth-tone hues throughout town. Add a charming waterfront location and a lot of pluck, and their efforts have succeeded beyond all expectations. The small burg has shops, restaurants, and 4 quality museums to while away some time. At the heart of La Conner's success is its focus on quality Northwest art. The town has a remarkable collection of outdoor sculptures that rotate annually and are for sale. Locate these pieces—there are usually about 2 dozen—by following the **La Conner Sculpture Walk,** which begins at the Chamber of Commerce building, located at 413 Morris St. While you are on Morris Street, stop at **Tillinghast Seed Company Inc.,** 623 Morris St. (360-466-3329 or

800-466-3329). The wooden porch overflows with potted flowers at this old-fashioned store, the oldest mail-order seed company in the Northwest. Inside you'll find seeds, plants, kitchen tools, country gifts, and spicy scents; upstairs there's a Christmas shop, and out in back a nursery in the shade of a tree that's a century and a half old—the largest European beech on the West Coast.

LUNCH **Kerstin's,** 505 S. 1st St.; (360) 466-9111. Open for lunch and dinner. The creative menu here includes wild salmon with lime butter sauce and local Samish Bay oysters, baked on the half shell. Lamb shanks prepared in a variety of ways also show up on the menu regularly.

First and Second Streets, above the harbor, are lined with antiques shops, boutiques, and art galleries. A sampling includes: **Earthenworks,** 713 1st St. (www.earthenworksgallery.com), showing top-quality Northwest ceramics, fabrics, watercolors, and photographs; **The Wood Merchant,** 709 S. 1st St. (360-466-4741; www.wood merchant.com), a Swinomish channelside showroom filled with the work of more than 200 American woodworkers; **Courtyard Gallery,** 701 S. 1st St. (360-466-1200; www.aclassactgallery.com), showing large and small high-quality art—sculptures, fountains, garden furniture, jewelry, and perfume bottles; **Homespun Market,** 622 S. 1st St. (360-466-4441), where European laces, hand-woven throws, and homespun fabrics are sold; and **The Scott Collection,** 512 S. 1st St. (360-630-9052; www.scottcollection.com), with Northwest pottery and porcelains, jewelry, bronze and brass sculpture, and numbered prints.

As you explore the town you'll see, just off Second Street, one of La Conner's oldest landmarks—a bank built in 1886, now the triangular-shaped city hall building. Near it is a pioneer home constructed in 1869 by Swedish immigrant Magnus Anderson. If you continue on Second Street you will reach the Gaches Mansion.

The **Gaches Mansion,** 703 S. 2nd St. (360-466-4288), is a 22-room structure that dates back to 1891. Once used as a hospital, the mansion has been restored and is open for tours on weekend afternoons. The **La Conner Quilt & Textile Museum** (360-466-4288; www.laconnerquilts.com/the-museum/gaches-mansion) is housed inside the Gaches Mansion—it's open Wednesday through Sunday and is said to be the only quilt museum in the United States.

Walk just 3 blocks to the **Museum of Northwest Art,** 121 S. 1st St. (360-466-4446; www.museumofnwart.org). The 12,000-foot contemporary building showcases past and present arts of the Pacific Northwest and is one of the few devoted solely to Northwest artists.

Four blocks in the opposite direction is the **Skagit County Historical Museum,** 501 4th St. (360-466-3365; www.skagit county.net/museum), which features exhibits showing life as it was in a previous century. Its windows frame views of the valley's fields with Mount Baker behind them.

DINNER   **Nell Thorn's Restaurant and Pub**, 205 E. Washington St.; (360) 466-4261; www.nellthorn.com/index.cfm. One of the town's consistently best restaurants, serving Northwest and French cuisine; with casual "pub grub" fare and entrees perfect for a special occasion. Fresh local seafood, pastas, and wines. Tables upstairs, cozy booths in the downstairs pub.

LODGING   **Wild Iris Inn,** 121 Maple Ave.; (360) 466-1400 or (800) 477-1400; www.wildiris.com. Always at the top of the list of most favored bed-and-breakfasts in western Washington, 18 rooms and suites in a 2-story Victorian style home. Guest and public dining Sun through Wed.

DAY 2 / MORNING

....

BREAKFAST   **Wild Iris Inn.** They serve you at your table for two, restaurant-style, and always offer fresh fruit, sometimes with yogurt, fresh-baked bread or pastry, and a warm entree, perhaps a spinach and mushroom crustless quiche.

You might rent a bicycle and take a ride in the country, passing fields green or ablaze with color; perhaps you'll see swans gliding through the marshes in the morning mist.

Alternatively, check the shops you missed yesterday. Walk through the **Butterfly Garden** on Second Street. If you're interested in antiques, La Conner has plenty to offer. **Morris Street Antique Mall,** 503 Morris St., carries a wide range of furniture, glassware, toys, and books. **Nasty Jack's,** 103 E. Morris St. (www.nastyjacks antiques.com), open daily, has a large selection of oak furniture.

AFTERNOON

....

Leaving La Conner, take Chilberg Road south to **Fir Island.** Less than a mile after you cross the bridge, the toasty scent of freshly baked waffle cones will draw you to **Snow Goose Produce,** 15170 Fir Island Rd. (360-445-6908). The open market sells produce, flowers, fresh seafood, and, the highlight, huge and delicious ice cream cones. They bake the hot waffle cones as you watch.

The Fir Island coast, along Skagit Bay, is ragged with islands and waterways, as the Skagit flows into the bay in a dozen places. Take exit 221 west to Fir Island Road, 1½ miles west of Conway. Meander through the new **Fir Island Farm/Hayton Reserve** and view the teeming wildlife at the mouth of Brown Slough. The Hayton grain fields are cut in November to provide food for the snow geese that arrive in late fall and stay through April; trumpeter and tundra swans and more than 70,000 ducks arrive each winter. Bald eagles, peregrine falcons, red-tailed hawks, and short-eared owls also feed and rest here. Paved parking and a ramp are available for universal access.

On Skagit City Road, take a peek at the tiny **Fir-Conway Lutheran Church,** which shelters a lovely sanctuary and a fine pipe organ. The congregation has roots dating back to 1888, when it first conducted services in a schoolhouse on Fir Island. In 1896 the congregation erected this small church building—just 24 by 42 feet and only 14 feet high. By 1916 the congregation had grown, and another church was built. In the following year, the Conway Norwegian Evangelical Lutheran Church united with the Fir church and became the Fir-Conway Lutheran Church. Close to the old church is **Larkspur Farm,** featured in *Country Living Gardener* magazine.

LUNCH Some say a visit to this area isn't complete without a stop at the friendly **Conway Pub and Eatery** in downtown Conway, 18611 Main St.; (360) 445-4733; www.theconwaypub.com, for a half-pound bacon cheeseburger, or a burger of chicken or grains. Wash it down with a brew or beverage that suits your fancy.

Back on Fir Island Road, head east across the Skagit to SR 530 and turn south. It's a few miles down the road to the small farming community of **Stanwood,** which was settled between 1870 and 1890. Called Centerville at the time, the community was the first Norwegian settlement in what is now Washington state. Stanwood's local history museum, the **D. O. Pearson (Pioneer) House and Museum,** 27108 102nd Ave. NW (360-629-6110), provides a comprehensive perspective of the region's development. Also worth the visitor's time is an easy and informative walk, best taken with the historical walking-tour guide published by the Stanwood Historical Society.

From Stanwood, drive to Silvana on SR 531. The pastoral valley is far more picturesque and relaxing than the freeway ride, and it doesn't add much time. You'll pass sprawling green fields and tidy plots, a red barn half-submerged in ivy, and a gray one with a moss-covered roof. A flag flies from the porch of an old-fashioned farmhouse, behind the lilacs.

About a half mile from Stanwood, you'll see a small white church on a hill. **Peace Lutheran Church**, built in 1884, is now a historic site, still in use and a favored location for weddings.

Blink as you enter the village of **Silvana,** on your way to join I-5, and you may miss it. Look for the **Little White Church on the Hill** off Pioneer Highway and the **Viking Hall,** part of the legacy of one of the largest Norwegian communities in the west and also a popular site for weddings.

Drive south on I-5 for the return to Seattle.

There's More . . . .

Gardens. **Christianson's Nursery,** 15806 Best Rd., Mount Vernon; (360) 466-3821 or (800) 585-8200; www.christiansonsnursery.com. Old Meadow School, built in 1888, sits on the nursery grounds, surrounded by rose and perennial gardens. The building is the site for a multitude of classes and social gatherings. An extensive gift shop is inside an old tractor garage.

Skagit Valley Bulb Farms, 15002 Bradshaw Rd., Mount Vernon; (360) 424-8152. Walk in fields of flowers, or take the Blue Trolley tour through the tulip fields. Have a picnic in the well-tended picnic area.

Washington State University Volunteer Display Gardens, 16650 Memorial Hwy., Mount Vernon; (360) 848-6120; www.mtvernon .wsu.edu/WSUmv/gardens.html. Open daily for self-guided tours. WSU Mount Vernon is on the left (south side of highway), ⅓ mile past the Avon Allen Road / SR 536 intersection.

Special Events . . . .

APRIL
Skagit Valley Tulip Festival, La Conner and Mount Vernon. Draws more than half a million people each year, to enjoy parades, flower shows, a street fair, a pancake breakfast, salmon barbecues, dances, pick-your-own and display flower fields, a food fair, and sports events (gymnastics, Slug Run). Park and ride to avoid traffic congestion. Make your hotel reservations early if you intend to stay in the area.

JUNE
La Conner Summer Street Festival. A celebration of La Conner art and history. Juried arts and craft shows. Food booths.

OCTOBER
Skagit Valley Festival of Family Farms. Visit 13 farms that include dairy, livestock, vegetables, and vineyards.

EARLY NOVEMBER
Art's Alive. For more than 2 decades, La Conner has paid its respects to regional culinary arts, music, and literature.

Other Recommended Restaurants and Lodging . . . .

LA CONNER
Calico Cupboard, 720 S. 1st St.; (360) 466-4451. Cafe that's famous for cinnamon rolls, muffins, breads, biscuits. Eat here, or take a pastry and coffee to go and eat by the water.

The Channel Lodge, 205 N. 1st St.; (360) 466-1500 or (888) 466-4113; www.laconnerlodging.com/laconner-channel-lodge.php. Stylish inn with country-contemporary decor. Forty rooms and 4 suites, all with fireplaces, most with harbor views.

Hotel Planter, 715 S. 1st St.; (360) 466-4710 or (800) 488-5409; www.hotelplanter.com. Twelve guest rooms with hand-crafted furniture in renovated vintage hotel. Private hot tub in garden.

La Conner Country Inn, 107 S. 2nd St.; (360) 466-3101 or (888) 466-4113; www.laconnerlodging.com/laconner-country-inn.php. Attractive 28-room inn with a country guest house theme. In the heart of town. Continental breakfast.

Seeds Bistro, 621 Morris St.; (360) 466-3280; www.seedsbistro .com. Serves breakfast, lunch, and dinner, and gives special recognition to children, with its "seedlings menu." The owners take advantage of the fresh seafood available to them, and make sure the menu offers foods that comfort (mac and cheese), and meals that surprise (steelhead with lavender compound butter).

MOUNT VERNON

Queen of the Valley Inn, 12757 Chilberg Rd.; (360) 466-4578 or (888) 999-1404; www.queenofthevalleyinn.com. Full gourmet breakfasts can include French toast bread pudding, roasted asparagus omelets, or poached eggs and ham.

For More Information . . . .

La Conner Chamber of Commerce, 606 Morris Street, P.O. Box 1610, La Conner, WA 98257; (360) 466-4778 or (888) 642-9284; www.laconner.net.

Mount Vernon Chamber of Commerce, 105 E. Kinkaid St., Mount Vernon, WA 98273; (360) 428-8547; www.mountvernonchamber.com.

NORTHBOUND ESCAPE *Two*
San Juan and Orcas Islands
BICYCLING NORTHWEST ISLANDS IN THE SUNSHINE /
2 NIGHTS

You will see all kinds of sea life when you ferry to the San Juan Islands: seagulls, whales, seals, eagles, boaters, fishers, islanders, and tourists in funny hats. With luck, you'll see some of the three pods of black-and-white orca whales that live year-round in these waters.

> Artisan galleries
> Ferry rides
> Historical museum and park
> Kayaking
> Scenic bay views
> Whale watching

Not all of the 172 islands of the San Juan Archipelago are accessible by ferry. We'll see the four biggest islands. Our Washington State ferry leaves from Anacortes, on Fidalgo Island, and stops at Orcas and Lopez Islands on its way to San Juan Island. Friday Harbor, on San Juan Island, is the only real town in the archipelago and has all the necessary facilities.

This escape is by car but can be adjusted for other transportation, including bicycle, taxi, and van shuttle. Go off-season or as a foot passenger to avoid long car-ferry waits in summer, when 50,000 island travelers swell to 250,000. Call (800) 84-FERRY for schedules.

DAY 1 / MORNING

From Seattle, drive north on I-5 for 60 miles. Continue west on SR 536 for 5 miles. Turn onto SR 20 west to Anacortes Ferry Terminal. Catch a ferry west for a 75-minute ride through island-dotted waters to **Orcas Island.** Orcas was named not for whales but for the

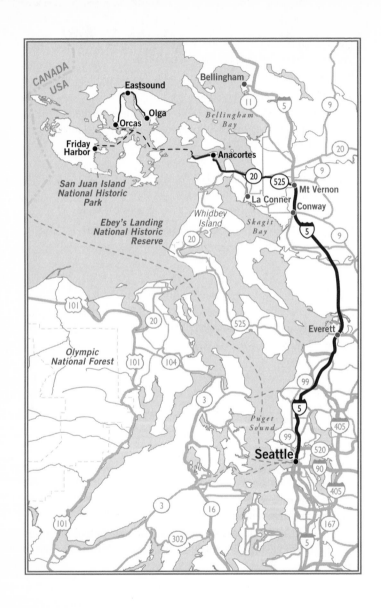

Mexican viceroy who charted the island along with Spanish explorer Francisco Eliza in 1791. He saw what you'll see, a 57-square-mile U-shaped island of thickly forested hills, with fjord-like inlets and 125 miles of pebbled shoreline.

Drive Horseshoe Highway 13 miles north from the ferry dock to **Eastsound,** a snug community at the head of the island's largest bay and the only commercial settlement.

Much of the valuable tribal collection housed in the **Orcas Island Historical Museum,** 181 N. Beach Rd. (360-376-4849; www.orcasmuseum.org) was saved by Ethan Allen, the San Juan Islands' superintendent of schools around the turn of the 20th century. His hand-built boat, used to row among the islands when he visited the schools, is in the exhibition, which is set in 6 homestead cabins.

LUNCH **Rose's Bakery and Cafe,** 382 Prune Alley, Eastsound; (360) 376-5805. Artisan breads are baked in-house, and their aromas waft through the cafe, which incorporates seasonal, local produce in soups, salads, and sandwiches. Located in the old Eastsound fire station next to Library Park.

AFTERNOON

Browse through Eastsound shops, especially **Darvill's Book Store,** 296 Main St. (360-376-2135), a combination bookstore–rare print shop. It's the oldest art gallery in the San Juan Islands and has an extensive collection of antique and contemporary prints. Just ¼ mile west off Horseshoe Highway is the **Howe Art Sculpture Park and Gallery** (360-376-2945; www.howeart.net; closed Mon), which features the large kinetic sculptures of Anthony Howe.

Visit Orcas's **Homegrown Market & Gourmet Deli,** 8 N. Beach Rd., Eastsound (360-376-2009) and pick up deli items and baked goods for a picnic dinner before you begin your afternoon drive on Horseshoe Bay.

Drive Horseshoe Highway 5 miles southeast to 5,175-acre **Moran State Park,** where a narrow, steep road leads another 5 miles to the top of **Mount Constitution,** the highest point in the San Juans, at 2,409 feet. From the 50-foot stone lookout tower, built in 1936 by the Civilian Conservation Corps, there's a see-forever view.

The forested mountain, lakes sparkling on its slopes, drops to a blue ocean. The archipelago of green islands stretches to the horizon. To the east, on the mainland, you can see the snowy peaks of **Mount Baker** and **Mount Rainier.**

An afternoon in or near the park can include biking, fishing, sailing, or kayaking. (See "There's More.") **Cascade Lake,** the biggest lake on the island, offers 3 campgrounds, a playground, picnic tables, restrooms, and rental boats. Swimming is good, but the area becomes crowded in summer.

Rent a rowboat and fish for trout in the stocked lake. Or hike the 2½-mile loop trail that starts west of the picnic area. It winds along a bluff above the lake, crosses a log bridge, and curves through forests of Douglas fir before circling back to the starting place. You may spy ducks, muskrat, otters, and great blue herons.

Continue east down Horseshoe Highway 2 miles beyond the state park to **Olga.** At **Orcas Island Artworks,** 11 Pt. Lawrence Rd. (360-376-4408), more than 50 artists display their wares daily March through December.

Or you can drive south past the Olga turnoff to Doe Bay Road and begin a kayaking adventure at **Doe Bay Village Resort and Retreat,** 107 Doe Bay Rd. (360-376-2291; www.doebay.com/index .html), where **Shearwater Sea Kayak Tours** (360-376-4699; www .shearwaterkayaks.com) offers several kayak trips for all skill levels. No experience is necessary. On one ride that's suitable for all ages, you'll paddle to **Doe Island Marine Park** and **Gorilla Rock,** returning via Rosario Strait. You're likely to spot dolphins, whales, and bald and golden eagles.

Follow the signs on Horseshoe Highway to **Rosario Resort,** which faces Cascade Bay on the edge of the sound. The centerpiece of the resort is the mansion built by Robert Moran, a shipbuilder and onetime mayor of Seattle. Consider attending an organ concert and a lively talk on the estate's history. Moran came here in 1905 thinking he had only a short time to live. In his 54-room home he installed a swimming pool, a bowling alley, and a music room containing an enormous pipe organ. Moran then lived on to a ripe old age. In 1920 he donated much of what is now Moran State Park to the state of Washington.

DINNER   **Rosario Resort,** 1400 Rosario Rd., Eastsound; (360) 376-2222 or (800) 562-8820; www.rosarioresort.com. Multilevel restaurant overlooking the sheltered waters of Cascade Bay. Serves a variety of American and continental dishes. Separate lounge on premises serves light meals and breakfast, lunch, and dinner.

LODGING   **Turtleback Farm Inn,** 1981 Crow Valley Rd.; (360) 376-4914 or (800) 376-4914; www.turtlebackinn.com. Take Horseshoe Highway back through Eastsound to this classic farmhouse-turned–country inn, the oldest lodging on the property that includes 7 comfortable rooms with private baths, common room with fireplace, and expansive deck overlooking 80 acres of pasture and woodland. The Orchard House is a new building with 4 guest rooms that sits in the center of an apple orchard on Turtleback Farm. All the guest rooms fill up quickly, so book yours early.

DAY 2 / MORNING

BREAKFAST   A full and fortifying breakfast at **Turtleback Farm Inn,** which includes fresh fruit and juices, an award-winning granola, homemade baked goods, and a meat and egg entree.

Take a scenic drive down Deer Harbor Road to the lighthouse, then circle back around West Sound and down Horseshoe Highway to the ferry terminal. Park your car and choose between 2 great morning adventures: biking and whale watching.

Orcas Island Eclipse Charters, at Orcas Ferry Landing on Orcas Island (360-376-6566 or 800-376-6566; www.orcasisland whales.com), tracks whales during its 3½-hour whale-watching trips that leave the Orcas Ferry Dock from 1:30 to 5 p.m. daily, March through October. Take this opportunity to see killer and minke whales, harbor seals, porpoises, bald eagles, ospreys, and other marine animals and wildlife. Pass by many of the spectacular 172 San Juan Islands. **Dolphin Bay Bicycles,** located at Orcas Ferry Landing (360-317-6734 or 360-376-4157; www.rockisland .com/~dolphin), and **Wildlife Cycles,** 350 N. Beach Rd., Eastsound (360-376-4708), rent bicycles. Island bicycle advocates recommend that travelers use less congested roads such as Crow Valley. For detailed public bicycle trail maps, view http://sanjuanisland trails.org/links, published by the San Juan Island Trails Committee.

LUNCH Have a bowl of seafood soup or a plate of fresh calamari at the historic **Orcas Hotel's cafe,** 18 Orcas Hill Rd.; (360) 376-4300 or (888) 672-2792; across the road from the ferry landing.

AFTERNOON

You will travel by ferry to **Friday Harbor,** a bustling wharfside village on San Juan Island. Ferry schedules change, so it's best to check times at www.wsdot.wa.gov/ferries. Walk-on passengers should arrive 15 minutes early, vehicles leaving in the morning 60 to 90 minutes early, and afternoon-departing vehicles from 2 to 4 hours early. To get your bearings, pick up maps and brochures at the visitor center in the Cannery Landing Building, next to the ferry harbor, just behind the open-air market.

For a casual in-town lunch with good salads, sandwiches, and baked goods, stop by the **Market Chef,** 225 A St. (360-378-4546), a deli 1 block from the ferry terminal that prepares made-to-order sandwiches and crisp salads, for dining in or taking out.

The **San Juan Island National Historic Park office,** 650 Mullis St., Suite 100 (360-378-2240; www.nps.gov/sajh; open daily in summer), and the **San Juan Island Historical Museum,** 405 Price St. (360-378-3949; www.sjmuseum.org; open 1 to 4:30 p.m. Wed through Sat in summer), offer historic exhibits that explain the island's contentious past and offer extensive oral-history collections of the island's Native Americans and Japanese settlers.

During the mid-1800s, Britain and the United States shared the island in an uneasy truce. When an American farmer shot a British pig that was disturbing his potato patch, the British authorities threatened to arrest the US citizen. The farmer appealed for help, and soon both sides were lined up for war (not solely because of the pig; San Juan Island has a most strategic location).

The dispute was settled peaceably, however, with the two camps establishing headquarters at opposite ends of the island. Through arbitration they finally agreed to American rule. Now the incident is remembered as the **Pig War.**

San Juan Transit (360-378-8887 or 800-887-8387; www.san juantransit.com) will take you on an island tour in season. **Susie's Mopeds,** 125 Nichols (360-378-5244 or 800-532-0087; www .susiesmopeds.com), just up from the ferry landing, rents mopeds by the hour or day. If you're driving yourself, head northwest for 10 miles on Roche Harbor Road to the remains of the **Roche Harbor Lime & Cement company town,** built in the late 1890s and now a historic complex with a resort, marina, cottages, and **Our Lady of Good Voyage Chapel,** the only privately owned Catholic church in the country.

Walk the docks and photograph the old church, and then turn south again to **British Camp,** at Garrison Bay. This portion of San Juan Island National Historical Park is where British troops were stationed during the infamous Pig War. Four restored buildings house interpretive exhibits. From the small formal garden, a trail rises to an overlook where officers were quartered.

Walk the **Bell Point Trail,** a level 1-mile hike above Garrison Bay, to reach a beach and a view of neighboring Westcott Bay. Or walk from the barracks exhibit to a cemetery for servicemen who died during the British occupation. Another ½-mile trail leads up 650-foot Mount Young for a far-reaching view of sea, scattered islands, and the Olympic and Cascade Mountains.

From British Camp, drive south to **Lime Kiln Point State Park,** where a trail leads to picturesque **Lime Kiln Lighthouse,** built in 1919 and now on the National Register of Historic Places.

Head south again to **Whalewatch Park,** the best location on the island to observe the 3 pods of black-and-white orcas that live in the waters around the San Juans. This is the nation's only whale-watching park. Signs and pictures tell you how to identify porpoises, orca, and minke whales.

If you sight whales, call the toll-free Whale Hotline (800-562-8832) in Washington. Reports of sightings help the Moclips Cetological Society to further its research.

Continue south to the southern tip of the island and **American Camp.** This section of the National Historical Park may seem bleak, with its windswept shores and open fields, but it, too, played an important part in island history. From the Exhibit Center an interpretive loop trail leads to the Officers' Quarters and the Hudson's Bay Company farm site. Farther down the road you'll find a parking area and several more walking paths. The hike to **Jakle's Lagoon,** along the old roadbed, passes through a grove of Douglas firs, and a walk up **Mount Finlayson** (290 feet high) presents another broad seascape and mountain vista.

On South Beach, the longest public beach on San Juan Island, birders will spot terns, plovers, greater and lesser yellowlegs, and bald eagles. Tide pools hold an abundance of marine life. You can salmon-fish from the beach if you have a license. Return to Friday Harbor.

DINNER   **Duck Soup Inn,** 50 Duck Soup Lane; (360) 378-4878; www .ducksoupinn.com. Fresh seafood and a varied wine list. Entree choices change regularly. Located north of town; closed in winter. **Vinny's Ristorante,** 165 West St.; (360) 378-1934; www.vinnysfridayharbor.com/index.html. Make reservations for a window seat, and feast on crab chiappino or tender calamari. An epicurean sensation, just perfect for a special occasion.

LODGING   **Longhouse Bed and Breakfast,** 2187 Mitchell Bay Rd.; (360) 378-2568; www.rockisland.com/~longhouse. Five rooms in a historic building that was a Native American longhouse. The space still exudes much of its dignity from yesteryear.

DAY 3 / MORNING

BREAKFAST   Guests at the **Longhouse** rave about the breakfasts, which begin with espresso drinks and homemade scones and continue with entrees such as quiche and locally made chicken sausage, and Dutch Baby pancakes with crème fraîche and fresh-cut strawberries. Dinner is also available with prior arrangement.

Visit the **Whale Museum,** 62 1st St. N, Friday Harbor (360-378-4710), one of the great attractions on the island. Life-size models of orca whales and numerous exhibits provide a quick education on whale life and habits.

Just down the street is the **Arctic Raven Gallery,** 130 1st St. S (360-378-3433 or 888-378-3222; www.arcticravengallery.com), with a collection of Northwest Coast Native masks, carvings, prints, jewelry, and baskets by master artists, as well as Inuit sculptures and prints. **Friday Harbor Art Studio,** 30 Web St. (360-378-5788; www.howardrosenfeld.com), is a back-street studio just 2 blocks away. Howard Rosenfeld's award-winning scrimshaw, jewelry, and engraved prints of marine subjects are on display here. **Island Studios,** 270 Spring St. (360-378-6550; www.islandstudios.com), represents over 120 artists from the San Juans. Local fine arts and crafts, such as original paintings, pottery, jewelry, prints, and art cards, are among the many quality items that make lovely gifts for friends back home. Clothing, weaving, etchings, glass art, and photography are also on display.

The **Island Dive and Watersports,** 2A Spring St. Landing (800-303-8386; www.divesanjuan.com), offers snorkeling and scuba-diving classes as well as charter diving boats and guides. You can also go whale watching, fishing, or sailing with various skippers who operate out of these docks. (See "There's More.")

LUNCH   **Downriggers Restaurant,** 10 Front St.; (360) 378-2700; www.downriggerssanjuan.com. Open every day for lunch and dinner. The restaurant specializes in seafood entrees but also prepares chicken and roast beef sandwiches and salads. Popular menu items include fish tacos, crab burgers, and a smoked salmon Reuben.

AFTERNOON

Watch for your ferry while you have lunch. Even though you haven't crossed the border to Canada, you can expect to pass through US Customs when you disembark from the 90-minute ferry ride. It's not a long process.

From Anacortes, drive east on SR 20 to I-5, or return to Seattle via Whidbey Island.

There's More . . . .

LOPEZ ISLAND
The ferry stops between Orcas and San Juan Islands at Lopez Island, which is popular with bicyclists because of its level roads.

Camping. **Spencer Spit State Park,** (360) 468-2251. The park's most notable feature is its ¼-mile sand spit that contains a saltwater lagoon marsh. This is one of the few state parks in the San Juan Islands that cars can access.

Kayaking. **Cascadia Kayak and Bike,** 135 Lopez Island; (360) 468-3008. This outlet offers visitors an opportunity to rent a kayak to explore the nearby bay. The company also offers guided trips and lessons.

Wildlife Viewing. **Shark Reef Sanctuary.** Visitors find impressive views of the San Juan Channel here, as well as have a chance to watch lounging seals and flitting seabirds, and explore life-rich tide pools.

ORCAS ISLAND
Airplane Rides. **Magic Air Tours Inc.,** Eastsound; (360) 376-2733 or (800) 376-1929; www.magicair.com. Scenic guided-tour flights with music in a yellow-and-red vintage biplane. Leather helmet, goggles, and scarf provided. Hangar with aeronautic memorabilia and hands-on activities for children.

Bicycling. **Island Bicycles,** 380 Argyle Ave., Friday Harbor; (360) 378-4941; www.islandbicycles.com.

Hiking. **Moran State Park,** www.stateparks.com/moran_san_juan .html. Has more than 30 miles of hiking trails, as well as waterfalls, and 5 lakes for boating.

Shopping. **Orcas Island Farmers' Market Association;** Village Green; Eastsound Village; (360) 472-1522; www.orcasislandfarmersmarket .org. Every Sat, May through mid-Oct. Homemade soaps, textiles, baskets, jewelry, candles, pottery, and fresh produce, of course.

Whale watching. **Deer Harbor Charters,** (360) 376-5989 or (800) 544-5758; www.deerharborcharters.com. You can sail bareboat or with a skipper, rent small boats by the hour or day, take a water taxi to any island destination, go whale watching, charter a guided fishing trip, or take a sunset cruise. A list of other whale-watching tours is available at www.gonorthwest.com/Washington/sanjuan/activities /whalelocal.htm.

SAN JUAN ISLAND

Air Transport. **Kenmore Air,** 6321 NE 175th St.; (425) 486-1257 or (800) 543-9595; www.kenmoreair.com. Flies to San Juan Islands from 2 Seattle locations, Kenmore and Port Angeles. PA is just two hours away.

Fishing. **Trophy Fishing Charters,** (360) 378-2110; www.fishthe sanjuans.com. Less than 2 minutes from the ferry landing. Half-day and multi-day trips.

Kayaking. **San Juan Kayak Expeditions,** 3090B Roche Harbor Rd., Friday Harbor; (360) 378-4436; www.sanjuankayak.com. Three- or 4-day sea-kayak expeditions around the San Juans and Canadian Gulf Islands.

San Juan Safaris, (360) 378-1323 or (800) 450-6858; www .sanjuansafaris.com. Leads whale-watching and kayaking trips Apr through Oct. Three- and 5-hour kayak tours in the San Juan Islands.

Sea Quest Kayak Expeditions, Friday Harbor; (360) 378-5767 or (888) 589-4253; www.sea-quest-kayak.com. Biologist guides on kayaks share their expertise on whales and Orcas tide-pool creatures. Half-day tours to Lime Kiln Whale Watch Park and 2- to 5-day camping trips to smaller islands.

Sailing Charters. **North Shore Charters,** Eastsound; (360) 376-4855. Fishing charters for ling cod, halibut, and rock fish, for up to 6 people.

Sail the San Juans, (360) 671-5852 or (800) 729-3207; www.sailthesanjuans.com. Six-day naturalist guided cruises exploring 200 islands. Biking and hiking opportunities, too.

Western Prince Cruises, Friday Harbor; (360) 378-5315 or (800) 757-6722. Call for hours. Narrated by Whale Museum naturalist.

Special Events . . . .

FOURTH OF JULY
Historical Day, Eastsound, Orcas Island. Parade, pancake breakfast, barbecue, music, fireworks.

AUGUST
Orcas Island Chamber Music Festival. World-class musicians performing in a series of concerts.

San Juan County Fair. Art exhibits, music, "trashion" show featuring recycled fashion wear. www.sanjuancountyfair.org.

SEPTEMBER
Anacortes Jazz Festival. Scenic wharfside concerts featuring top-notch jazz talent and local seafood.

Lopez Island Annual Artists Studio Tour. Self-guided tour of 25 studios. Some artists demonstrate their techniques.

OCTOBER
Fall Festival of the Arts. Open studios, galleries and music. www.art stocksanjuanisland.com.

Other Recommended Restaurants and Lodging . . . .

ORCAS ISLAND
Kangaroo House Bed & Breakfast, 1459 North Beach Rd., Eastsound; (888) 371-2175; www.kangaroohouse.com. Located 1 mile north of central Eastsound. Three rooms, 2 suites, in a Craftsman-style bungalow. Multicourse breakfast. Hot tub in a garden that's been certified as a Backyard Wildlife Sanctuary.

Kingfish Inn, 4362 Crow Valley Rd., Eastsound; (360) 376-4440; www.kingfishinn.com. Three rooms and a suite and the adjacent Kingfish Inn Dining Room, serving breakfasts, salads, and small plates.

New Leaf Cafe, 171 Main St., Eastsound; (360) 376-2200; www .outlookinn.com/dining.htm. Located in The Outlet Inn. Breakfasts and dinners are varied and innovative: seafood omelets, smoked salmon Benedict, wild salmon with pear-ginger glaze, and grilled halibut with slow-roasted yellow tomato relish. Lovely ambience.

Orcas Hotel, 8 Orcas Hill Rd., Orcas; (360) 376-4300 or (888) 672-2792; www.orcashotel.com/index.html. Remodeled 12-room historic hotel with Victorian flavor. Overlooks ferry landing. On the premises is Octavia's Bistro, a steak and seafood restaurant.

Otters Pond Bed and Breakfast, 100 Tomihi Dr., Eastsound; (360) 376-8844 or (888) 893-9680; www.otterspond.com. Six rooms with private baths overlook a pond and wetlands. Amenities such as thick bathrobes, a hot tub, library, and an exquisite garden create a quiet and comfy respite for visitors. Each day begins with a lavish 5-course breakfast.

Rosario Resort, 1400 Rosario Rd., Eastsound; (360) 376-2222 or (800) 562-8820; www.rosarioresort.com. Has a number of suites and waterfront king rooms. Former private estate on gorgeous Cascade Bay. Rooms in outlying buildings have basic motel amenities; the mansion has a restaurant and lounge, indoor and outdoor pools, and spa facilities.

FRIDAY HARBOR

Argyle House Bed and Breakfast, 685 Argyle Ave.; (360) 378-4084 or (800) 624-3459; www.argylehouse.net, within walking distance of Friday Harbor town, in private setting with goldfish pond and fountain. Two cottages and 3 rooms. A large hot tub for soaking at the end of the day. Breakfast consists of fresh-baked muffins and a hot entree.

Backdoor Kitchen & Catering, 400 A St.; (360) 378-9540; www .backdoorkitchen.com. This establishment specializes in what it calls "ethnic menus," presented in surprising ways, such as Thai-style fried tofu with yams, Mediterranean lamb sirloin with gremolata, and crepes with parsley-almond pesto and Gruyère, served with lentils.

Clay Cafe, 10 1st St. N; (360) 378-5544. Sells espresso, baked goods. Living up to its name, the cafe offers ceramic-ware for purchase.

The Dragonfly Inn, 4770 Roche Harbor Rd.; (360) 378-4280 or (877) 378-4280; www.thedragonflyinn.com. Inn decorated with Japanese fabrics, furnishings, and mats, and serving Asian fusion breakfasts.

Lonesome Cove, 416 Lonesome Cove Rd.; (360) 378-4477; www .lonesomecove.com. Secluded retreat with 7 hand-built log cabins, on Speiden Channel.

Maloula's Restaurant, 1 Front St.; (360) 378-8485; www.maloula .com. Located on the rooftop of the Town Square building. Open for lunch and dinner. Serves Mediterranean cuisine with vegan, meat, and seafood options.

Olympic Lights, 146 Starlight Way; (360) 378-3186 or (888) 211-6195; www.olympiclights.com. Bed-and-breakfast in 1895 farmhouse on 5 acres at the south end of the island. Three rooms with contemporary furnishings, white carpets. Full vegetarian breakfast included.

Trumpeter Inn Bed and Breakfast, 318 Trumpeter Way; (360) 378-3884 or (800) 826-7926; www.trumpeterinn.com. Quiet country inn of charm and grace, nestled in lush gardens. Several rooms recently remodeled; 1 is wheelchair accessible. Full breakfast.

Wildwood Manor, 5335 Roche Harbor Rd.; (360) 378-3447 or (877) 298-1144; www.wildwoodmanor.com. Surrounded by forest, wildlife, and San Juan Channel water views. Sits on 9 acres, with immense lawns and lovely gardens. Impeccably decorated rooms. Three-course breakfast includes homemade baked goods, fresh fruit, and a hot entree.

For More Information . . . .

Orcas Island Chamber of Commerce, 65 North Beach Rd., Eastsound, WA 98245; (360) 376-2273; www.orcasislandchamber.com

San Juan Island Chamber of Commerce, 135 Spring St., Friday Harbor, WA, 98250; (360) 378-5240; www.sanjuanisland.org.

Washington State Ferries, 2901 3rd Ave., Suite 500, Seattle, WA 98121; out-of-state (206) 464-6400 or (888) 808-7977; www .wsdot.wa.gov/ferries. The ferries all depart from Pier 52.

NORTHBOUND ESCAPE *Three*

Vancouver, British Columbia

SAVORING MULTICULTURAL DELIGHTS IN VANCOUVER /
2 NIGHTS

Cosmopolitan shopping
Granville Island
International cuisine
Marine Science Center
Queen Elizabeth Park and
Bloedel Conservatory

Vancouver, British Columbia, is a dazzling city on the Georgia Strait, its mirror-facade skyscrapers reflecting billowy cloud formations and jagged snow-covered peaks in the distance. To visit Vancouver is to visit a half-dozen cultures at once. Aboriginal peoples and immigrants from India, China, and Vietnam have all settled in Vancouver city and its environs. Walks through their bustling neighborhoods should be a required stop for any traveler who appreciates restaurants that waft aromatic spices and shops that carry exotic cooking vessels, clothing, and jewelry.

Vancouver's spectacular waterfront, ethnic diversity, and cultural venues are all reasons why Canada's westernmost province consistently rates as one of the top cities in the Americas to visit, in the annual *Condé Nast Traveler* awards. This escape takes you by Quick Shuttle bus, on which you can sit back and enjoy the scenery through northern Washington and the Peace Arch International Park at the British Columbia border. Quick Shuttle provides complimentary doorstep service to all major Vancouver hotels.

Robson Street's trendy shops along the 3-block stretch between Burrard and Jervis is a commercial mecca that includes premier fashions stores, fine dining, and a proximity to the world-class anthropology museum at the **University of British Columbia** campus. There's also the **Morris and Helen Belkin Art Gallery** and botanical gardens, and the 9-mile **Pacific Spirit Regional Park** that

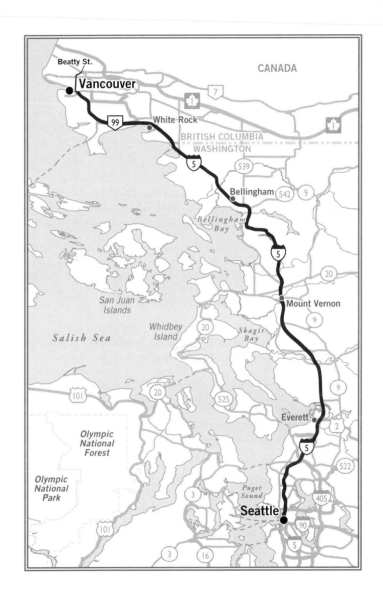

abuts the shoreline of the Georgia Strait. The park's forests stretch across Point Grey, separating the city from the University of British Columbia. Yet the park is close enough to entice students and city dwellers on foot and by bus and bike.

DAY 1 / AFTERNOON

You will leave Seattle by Quick Shuttle (800-665-2122; www .quickcoach.com), a transportation service that offers 5 departure times by bus each day to Vancouver, B.C., departing either from the Sea-Tac Airport or downtown Seattle. The 3½-hour ride ends in downtown Vancouver, where it stops at several hotels, including the Georgian Court.

After disembarking Quick Shuttle, leave your bags at your hotel (the Georgian Court Hotel Vancouver) and walk to your lunch destination.

LUNCH **Cafe Medina,** near the Georgian Court Hotel, 556 Beatty St.; (604) 879-3114; www.medinacafe.com. Open daily for both breakfast and dinner, a fine blending of French, Spanish, and Moroccan menu items.

Get your bearings after lunch by taking the hop-on, hop-off **Vancouver Trolley Company,** 875 Terminal Ave. (888-451-5581; www .vancouvertrolley.com) tour, noting attractions that suit your fancy so you can go back later and spend more time. The tour lasts about 2½ hours and allows visitors to hop off at any of the 29 or so stops to visit the attractions. After the tour, if you are ready to put your feet up, you can dine at the Beatty Street Bar & Grill inside the Georgian Court Hotel or you can hop in a taxi or walk to dinner.

DINNER **Joe Fortes Seafood & Chop House,** 777 Thurlow St.; (604) 669-1940; www.joefortes.ca. The restaurant is large, and the booths are cozy. The mezzanine above gives a bird's-eye view of all the action. Serves more than 50 types of fresh fish as well as a few steak and chop dishes. Delectable desserts that are beautiful to look at.

LODGING **Georgian Court Hotel Vancouver,** 773 Beatty St.; (604) 682-5555; www.georgiancourthotelvancouver.com. A hotel that's European in style and warmly Canadian in hospitality. The Georgian Court is located in the heart of downtown Vancouver and is within walking distance of all major attractions. Guests can choose among 4 quality on-site restaurants.

Nearby, the **Vancouver Public Library,** modeled on the Coliseum in Rome, is just 2 blocks from the hotel. Poetry readings and other literary events take place almost daily (often in the evening) and are generally free.

DAY 2 / MORNING

BREAKFAST **The Bistro,** in the Georgian Court Hotel, offers its guests a large hot breakfast buffet that includes eggs, pancakes, fruits, and juices.

Don't miss the **University of British Columbia Museum of Anthropology,** 6393 NW Marine Dr. (604-822-5087; www.ubc.ca). Buses leave from the downtown Granville Mall to the Botanical Gardens on Marine Drive, or the Museum of Anthropology on Point Grey Cliffs (www.ubc.ca/about/maps.html). This teaching and research museum is renowned for its displays of world arts and cultures, especially works by First Nations peoples of the Pacific Northwest coast. You will find magnificent examples of works in red cedar, originating from several First Nations communities, including the Haida, Kwakwaka'wakw, Gitxsan, Nisga'a, Haisla, and Oweekeno. The **Haida House** complex, located outside the museum (and visible from the Great Hall), includes structures that would have been present in a 19th-century Haida village. Constructed in 1962, the complex includes a large family dwelling and a smaller mortuary house similar to those typically used to hold the dead.

For high-quality gifts, visit the **UBC Museum of Anthropology Museum Shop** (www.moa.ubc.ca/shop/index.php). Attractive T-shirts with First Nations and nature motifs, jewelry, art cards, ceramics, and a wide variety of First Nations and art books.

Have lunch at an upscale but unpretentious bistro on campus.

LUNCH **The Sage Bistro,** 6331 Crescent Rd.; (604) 822-0968; www .sage.ubc.ca. Imaginative food surrounded by art-deco architectural details and views from floor-to-ceiling windows. Although the prices might be higher than at most university dining rooms open to the public, the cost for your lunch will prove reasonable given the quality of the pan-roasted Coho salmon and grilled rib eye with Szechwan peppercorn glace. Or you can just stop here for a coffee break and have lunch at one of the many casual eateries in the surrounding neighborhood.

AFTERNOON

Less than a mile from downtown, **Stanley Park** (http://vancouver .ca/parks/parks/stanley) is loved by Vancouverites as an oasis from urban intensity. Visitors appreciate this city forest, too. Eighty percent of its trees are coniferous, creating a year-round emerald haven for walkers and bicyclists, and most of the park is surrounded by water. Inside the park are too many sites to list, but highlights include the award-winning **Woodland Wildflower Garden** with 200 species of wildflowers and ferns native to North America. Other specialty gardens include the **Evelyn B. Rose Garden** and a colorful, fragrant **herb garden.** Kids love to visit the **children's farmyard,** home to more than 100 animals. Pot-bellied pigs, goats and sheep mingle easily with passers-by. The **Vancouver Aquarium Marine Science Center** (www.vanaqua.org) is home to 70,000 animals, making it Canada's largest. It's open every day. Inside there's the Upstream Cafe and a gift shop, and the hands-on Clownfish Cove for children.

It's about a 15-minute taxi ride from Stanley Park to the **False Creek AquaBus** (604-689-5858; www.theaquabus.com), which provides service to and from **Granville Island;** the Aquabus runs daily from 9 a.m. to 7 p.m., approximately every 20 minutes. Also, the number 19 bus runs from the park to downtown, where you can hop on the AquaBus.

Forty years ago, the Granville Island infrastructure was deteriorating, and most of the industrial spaces were vacant. Today, thanks to the government's interest in creating a public-friendly space, the old warehouses are still there, but inside are galleries, studios, and restaurants. Take some time browsing a bookstore, the craft shops, the fresh produce at the sparkling clean **Granville Public Market,** then have a break at **La Baguette & L'Echalote,** 1680 Johnston St. (604-684-1351; www.labaguette.ca/home.html), with a fine selection of French terrines and pâtés, duck legs, and lamb shanks, as well as cream pastries, croissants, artisan breads, and baguette sandwiches. Assemble to-go items for a dinner in your room or leave Granville and head across the bridge for a seafood dinner.

DINNER   Go Fish Ocean Emporium, 1505 1st Ave. W; (604) 730-5040. Looks so casual, you might be surprised at how tasty the halibut and chips and fish tacos and coleslaw are.

LODGING   Georgian Court Hotel Vancouver.

DAY 3 / MORNING

....

| BREAKFAST | The Bistro, in the Georgian Court Hotel. |

You can take a Quick Shuttle at noon and be back in downtown Seattle by 4 p.m.

There's More . . . .

Art galleries. **Bill Reid Gallery of Northwest Coast Art,** 639 Hornby St.; (604) 682-3455; www.billreidgallery.ca. An impressive collection of metalwork by Reid, including a 27-foot bronze frieze. Reid is considered one of Canada's great contemporary artists. The gallery also has a gift shop with high-quality art, starting at reasonable prices.

Vancouver Art Gallery, 750 Hornsby St., (604) 662-4700. The largest Canadian art museum west of Toronto and the fourth-largest in Canada. An especially fine exhibition of the work of Canadian artist Emily Carr.

Boat tours. **Vancouver Boat Tours,** 103-388 Drake St.; (604) 329-4467; www.vancouverboattours.com. These tours invariably meet or exceed visitor expectations. The company operates year-round, offering full- and half-day tours of the city harbor and Howe Sound, and surroundings.

Gardens. **Nitobe Memorial Garden.** Near the entrance of the University of British Columbia. The cherry blossoms are in bloom in April and May, but this garden is beautiful any time of the year.

Queen Elizabeth Park and Bloedel Conservatory, at Cambie Street and W. 33rd Ave. or 4600 Cambie St.; (604) 257-8570; www .vancouver.ca/parks/parks/queenelizabeth/index.htm. Once home to a massive quarry, now swathed with 130 acres of lush gardens, on and around the 492-foot-high Little Mountain. Make time for the extensive outdoor arboretum and the indoor Bloedel Floral Conservatory with exotic birds, fish, and tropical flowers. The projectile-like dancing fountain, with 70 jets using 23,000 gallons of recirculating water, dances nonstop.

Museums. **Roedde House Museum,** 1415 Barclay St.; (604) 684-7040; www.roeddehouse.org/home.php. A late-Victorian home in the Queen Anne revival-style that was built in 1893 for the family of immigrant Gustav Roedde. Visitors have an opportunity to walk through every room and even handle some of the artifacts that reflect the quotidian life of the middle class in Vancouver.

Special Events . . . .

JUNE THROUGH SEPTEMBER
Bard on the Beach. Western Canada's largest professional Shakespeare festival. All productions presented in Vanier Park on Vancouver's waterfront. The Main Stage has 520 seats and the Douglas Campbell Studio Stage provides 240 seats. For tickets, call (604) 739-0559 or go to www.bardonthebeach.org.

JULY
Celebration of Light, English Bay. At the heart of this event is the international pyro-musical fireworks competition, considered the largest of its kind in the world. Countries around the globe compete before an audience of more than 1.4 million spectators.

Vancouver Folk Music Festival, (604) 602-9798; www.atthefestival .bc.ca. High-quality performances in an outdoor setting.

Vancouver International Jazz Festival, (604) 872-5200 or (888) 438-5200; www.coastaljazz.ca. The Coastal Jazz and Blues Society has been organizing this event for more than 25 years, sharing with grateful audiences a variety of jazz, blues, world, and improvised music concerts.

JULY THROUGH AUGUST

Theatre Under the Stars, (713) 558-2600; www.tuts.com. For more than 40 years, this musical theater company has been performing top-notch Disney and Broadway productions.

OCTOBER

Vancouver International Film Festival. Provided by the Greater Vancouver International Film Festival Society, the event screens Canadian and international films by younger filmmakers. In a typical year, viewers can expect to see films representing more than 50 countries.

Other Recommended Restaurants and Lodging . . . .

Arbutus Vista Vancouver Bed and Breakfast Suite, 2172 W. 22nd Ave.; (604) 603-7289; www.vancouverbnb.com. You are the only guests in your 548-foot self-contained suite, and a breakfast is delivered to you each morning.

Caffè Artigiano, 763 Hornby St.; (604) 990-0542; http://caffe artigiano.com. You'll find CA cafes in several locations in Vancouver. Very popular with locals who crave a good cup of coffee.

Corkscrew Inn, 2735 W. Second Ave.; (604) 733-7276; www .corkscrewinn.com. Four rooms decorated tastefully in individual themes in a carefully redesigned Craftsman-style home, with reused or restored original material. One and a half blocks from the beach. Full gourmet breakfast might include salmon frittata, lemon ricotta pancakes, and tomato tarts or a later and lighter self-serve breakfast. Finally, an extensive collection of corkscrews from the 18th and 19th centuries.

Diva at the Met, 645 Howe St.; (604) 602-7788; www.metropolitan .com/diva. Open for breakfast, lunch, and dinner, inside the Metropolitan Hotel. There's roasted halibut, grilled flatiron steak, or cinnamon smoked duck breast. Maybe you just want dessert after an evening at the theater. Try Diva's warm chocolate soufflé cake. Fine place for special occasions.

Frenchies Diner, 425 Dunsmuir St.; (604) 253-4545; www.frenchies-diner.com. Open every day from 11 a.m. to 4 p.m. Traditional French Canadian food, such as tourtière (meat pie), poutine (fries, cheese curds, gravy), and maple sugar pie, and Montreal smoked meat sandwiches.

Le Bistro de Paris, 751 Denman St.; (604) 681-6550; www.lebistro deparis.com/index.html. Lunch "plats de principaux" range from omelets with fries to steak frites and lots of other French bistro favorites in between, while dinners include coquilles St. Jacques and filet mignon.

Light Heart Inn Bed & Breakfast, 2118 E. 10th Ave.; (604) 299-5993 or (877) 299-5993; www.lightheartinn.ca. In the "Commercial Drive" area known for its many Italian and Mediterranean restaurants. Within minutes of Chinatown. Three large rooms, each with private bathrooms. Full breakfasts can include French toast, huevos rancheros, and homemade corn bread.

Nelson House Bed & Breakfast, 977 Broughton St.; (604) 684-9793 or (866) 684-9793; www.nelsonhousebb.com. Five rooms with different moods, ranging from ultraromantic to a woodsy wood-paneled room with a stove to warm you after a misty Vancouver day. Only a 10-minute walk from Stanley Park, where you will find 1,000 acres of forests and beaches to stroll or bicycle across.

Olympia Oyster & Fish Company, 820 Thurlow St.; (604) 685-0716. Said to serve Vancouver's best fish (sole, halibut, and cod) and chips. Best to take it away, because there are only a few tables and countertop seats for dining.

Robson Suites, 777 Bidwell St., West End; (604) 685-9777 or (800) 404-1398; www.robsonsuitesvancouver.com. Situated in the picturesque West End of downtown near Stanley Park, the Vancouver Aquarium, and the beautiful beaches of English Bay. This is an apartment-style property, fully furnished with kitchens, refrigerators, microwaves, dishwashers, washers, dryers, and free gated underground parking.

Rogue Kitchen & Wetbar, 601 West Cordova St., Waterfront Station, Gastown; www.roguewetbar.com. A variety of salads, pastas, salmon and chicken sandwiches, and pizza. Open for lunch and dinner. Sand-blasted brick and well-worn hardwood floors make this a comfortable place to sit down for a lower-cost lunch or dinner.

West End Guest House, 1362 Haro St.; (888) 546-3327; www .westendguesthouse.com. Located in Vancouver's downtown West End, this establishment gives visitors easy access to shops, restaurants, and Stanley Park. Each room has its own private bathroom, cable TV, and DVD player. One of Vancouver's tour companies can pick you up in front of the Guest House to show you the sights.

Bicycles are available free to guests. Full gourmet breakfast and complimentary refreshments.

For More Information . . . .

Amtrak, 303 S. Jackson St.; (800) 872-7245; www.amtrakcascades .com. The train departs Seattle each day at 7:40 a.m. from the historic King Street Station in Pioneer Square and transfers travelers to an Amtrak bus, which arrives in Vancouver at 11:35 a.m. at the Pacific Central Station, 1150 Station St.

Quick Shuttle, Main Terminal Building, 17801 Pacific Hwy. S, Seattle; reservations, (800) 665-2122; www.quickcoach.com/contact .htm. Offers several departure times from Sea-Tac Airport to downtown Vancouver. Approximately 4½ hours; $74 round-trip.

Tourism Vancouver, Greater Vancouver Convention and Visitors Bureau, 200 Burrard St., Suite 210, Vancouver, British Columbia, Canada V6C 3L6; (604) 682-2222; www.tourismvancouver.com/ visitors.

Washington and British Columbia Border Information, 120-176th St., Suite 101, Surrey, B.C.; (604) 538-1042 or (800) 663-4270; www.borderlineups.com.

NORTHBOUND ESCAPE *Four*
Whistler, British Columbia
ASCENDING BRITISH COLUMBIA'S SEA-TO-SKY
CORRIDOR / 2 NIGHTS

> Bald eagles
> Bicycle paths
> First Nations history and art
> Hiking trails
> Mining museum
> Olympic-caliber ski resort

In this escape, a 4- to 5-hour drive from Seattle, you will travel along Highway 99, called the Sea to Sky Highway. Those who venture on this 2-day escape to Whistler, B.C., will be surprised at the astonishing array of historic sites and geologic viewpoints along the way, beginning at Horseshoe Bay and ending at Whistler, at which point you will have climbed from sea level to 2,200 feet. And what views you will have along the way.

You will drive on I-5 north from Seattle to Blaine, where you will cross the border into British Columbia and pass the Peace Arch International Park. Perhaps you have already taken the Vancouver escape and are ready to continue driving north on Highway 99 north to Whistler, your destination for the next 2 nights.

The Coast Salish First Nations were the first to occupy these majestic mountains and fertile valleys. British naval officers didn't arrive until centuries later, when they first surveyed the area around Whistler in the 1860s. They originally called Whistler "London Mountain." But after trappers, miners, and loggers inhabited the region in the early 1900s, they called the area Whistler, after the whistle sound of a ground squirrel called a hoary marmot—sometimes called a whistle pig—that lived in the rocks.

It wasn't until 1962 that two businessmen came up with the idea to develop the area into a ski resort, and ultimately, the winter Olympic Games. Whistler officially opened in 1966, and Blackcomb in 1980.

Along the Sea to Sky Corridor, you will be able to trace the area's cultural history in a succinct way, with 7 interpretive cultural kiosks the shape of cedar-bark hats. You will find the first five on the drive north, and southbound you will see numbers 6 and 7.

When you are planning your trip, study the Whistler lodging addresses with care. Some visitors have the best experience staying close to Whistler Village, in close proximity to many shops and cafes, and night activities. Others have a more memorable stay away from the village activity, savoring a deeper outdoor experience.

In preparation for the Winter Olympics in February 2010, Whistler ramped up its accommodations and choices of eateries, which new visitors continue to benefit from.

DAY 1 / MORNING

In North Vancouver, visit the **Capilano Suspension Bridge,** one of the area's oldest attractions. Originally built in 1889, the Capilano Suspension Bridge (604-985-7474; www.capbridge.com) swings 450 feet across and 230 feet above the Capilano River. These days the bridge is just one attraction in the 27-acre **Capilano Suspension Bridge Park.** One attraction is **Treetops Adventure,** said to be the first of its kind in North America, offering a lofty view of the coastal forest. Visitors move from one Douglas fir tree to another on a series of elevated suspension bridges, some reaching 100 feet above the forest floor. Free guided tours are offered every hour all year-round and every half hour during the summer months. If you arrive in time for lunch, the park offers 3 dining options: the pioneer-themed **Loggers' Grill,** the casual **Canyon Cafe,** and the full-service **Bridge House Restaurant.**

Take Highway 99 20 miles to Horseshoe Bay (www.horseshoe baybc.ca/horseshoebaytourism.htm), a picturesque seaside village at the entrance of Howe Sound, on the northwestern side of Vancouver, and the official start of the Sea to Sky Highway, as well as where Highway 1 (Trans-Canada) and Highway 99 (Sea to Sky) meet. A waterfront playground makes this a scenic stop for kids and parents, who can read cultural kiosk number 1. The next attraction is **Porteau Cove Provincial Park** (www.env.gov.bc.ca/bcparks/explore/parkpgs/porteau), which is not only a popular scuba-diving destination, but an alcove rich in marine life species.

Right on Highway 99 at **Britannia Beach** is the **Britannia Mine Museum** (800-896-4044; www.bcmm.ca), exhibiting the history of what was the largest copper-producing mine in the British Commonwealth. Now you can explore historic buildings, board a mining train, and travel through an old mining tunnel. The entire museum site is like an open-air museum, with historical machinery, from mucking machines to ore carts and a working lime tank. The 1908 Machine Shop holds a number of historic pieces of equipment, including a restored ambulance car, and the "man car" that squeezed 16 miners into a vehicle about the size of a small family car. There is also a visitor center, the Chatterbox Gift Shop, with gifts and souvenirs, and a playground.

This is where you will find cultural kiosk 2. Stop by the **CRS Trading Post** in Britannia Beach (604-896-0001; www.thecrstradingpost.com/index.html) for authentic, high-quality art by Coast Salish natives of the Squamish nations. You'll find paintings, masks, jewelry, shoes, hats, and native dolls.

After you leave Britannia, you will pass **Murrin Provincial Park** (www.env.gov.bc.ca/bcparks/explore/parkpgs/murrin.html), well known for its rock-climbing opportunities for beginners and experts alike. At **Shannon Falls Provincial Park** (www.env.gov.bc.ca/bcparks/explore/parkpgs/shannon.html), you might want to take an easy trail up to the viewpoint and allow yourself to become mesmerized by the 1,099-foot falls, among the largest in British Columbia.

You probably won't miss **Stawamus Chief Provincial Park** (www.env.gov.bc.ca/bcparks/explore/parkpgs/stawamus), where the world's second-largest granite monolith, **Stawamus Chief Mountain,** resides. It rises 2,297 feet and has long been the nesting site for the protected peregrine falcon. Even if you aren't a climber who dares to climb the sheer vertical face of this rock, you can still find stunning views of Howe Sound and the Squamish Valley. At kiosk number 3, you will learn about Stawamus Chief and Shannon Falls.

Now you are in **Squamish,** halfway between Vancouver and Whistler and the "outdoor recreation capital" of Canada. Here windsurfers ride the air's movement at **Squamish Spit.** The area also has outlets for hiking, rock climbing, kite boarding, and cross-country mountain biking on 600 trails through old-growth forest, which are accessible year-round in the provincial park. Visitors who are unable or don't care to engage in rigorous activity can marvel at the natural beauty of the Squamish Valley. You'll find kiosk number 4 at the **Squamish Adventure Centre,** a building that houses visitor information, the Squamish Chamber of Commerce, a theater featuring tourism videos, and a cafe.

Hop farms flourished in the Squamish Valley, and it's apropos to have a brewing company and pub right in the center of town that serves a wide variety of microbrews.

LUNCH   Try the **Howe Sound Inn and Brewing Co.,** 37801 Cleveland Ave., Squamish; (604) 892-2603; www.howesound.com. This is a good choice for microbrew lovers and visitors who enjoy Canadian cuisine. The Howe Sound Inn also offers pleasant accommodations and provides a fabulous view of "the Chief." Children are welcome in the patio dining area. If the family wants a simple meal of bagels and cream cheese or sandwiches, head over to the **Sunflower Bakery Cafe,** 38086 Cleveland Ave.; (604) 892-2231; www.sunflowerbakerycafe.com/map.html. Treat yourselves to pie, flan, or a slice of torte for dessert.

AFTERNOON

After lunch, stroll through a few Squamish art galleries. The **Squamish Native Art Store,** 37991B Cleveland Ave. (604-892-2349; www.squamishnativeartstore.com), sells a fine selection of aboriginal Pacific Northwest carvings, jewelry, and masks by Native Canadians. The **Foyer Gallery** at the Squamish Public Library, 37907 Second Ave. (604-892-3110; www.squamish.bclibrary.ca/services-programs /foyer-gallery) regularly features the work of local artists.

Brackendale is winter home to the bald eagle, boasting the largest gathering of bald eagles in North America, from November through February (www.brackendaleeagles.com). The local art gallery sponsors the annual eagle count each January, drawing international crowds. The best viewing is at "Eagle Run," along the city marsh, which has a walking trail and a viewing platform and is reached by leaving the highway at Mamquam Road and heading north on Government Road. In 2010, 956 birds were counted, an appreciable decrease from 1994, when the count was 3,769.

Stop by the **Alexander Falls and Interpretive Forest,** an easily accessible recreation site, then stop at the **Whistler Interpretive Forest Recreation Site** (www.for.gov.bc.ca/dsq/interpForests /interpretive.htm#Whistler_Interpretive_Forest), where you will find cultural kiosk 5.

With 8,100 acres of skiable terrain, **Whistler** is the largest ski area in North America. Located northwest of Garibaldi Provincial Park in the Fitzsimmons Range of British Columbia's coastal mountains, it was the perfect home for the 2010 Olympic Games.

The **Peak 2 Peak Gondola,** opened in 2008, travels across the valley between Whistler (7,160 feet) and Blackcomb (7,494 feet), and is the world's longest continuous lift system. Rising 1,427 feet above the valley floor, the gondola transports skiers, snowboarders, hikers, and sightseers alike, taking them the 2.73 miles between the two mountains in 11 minutes. There are 18 hiking and walking trails on both mountains.

From mid-May through mid-September, visitors gaze awe-struck at the 360-degree view of Whistler and Blackcomb's alpine landscape. This is the time of year to access the 20 hiking trails on both mountains.

DINNER **Ciao-Thyme Bistro,** 4573 Chateau Blvd.; (604) 932-9795 www.ciaothymebistro.com. Open daily for breakfast, lunch, and dinner. Famous for the roasted carrot and Brie soup and yam fries. High-quality, innovative menu.

LODGING **Chalet Luise Bed & Breakfast Inn,** 7461 Ambassador Crescent, Whistler; (604) 932-4187 or (800) 665-1998; www.chaletluise.com. Within walking distance of Whistler Village. Eight rooms with private bathrooms, including twins and kings. Jacuzzi overlooking gardens; sauna, too.

DAY 2 / MORNING

BREAKFAST **Chalet Luise Bed & Breakfast Inn** serves a buffet-style continental breakfast and daily hot option, such as poached eggs or blueberry waffles.

Bike riding is one of the most popular outdoor activities at Whistler. After breakfast, begin your day with a bike ride in **Lost Lake Park,** with dozens of trails composing a 20-mile network, and something for every level of bicyclist. The park is right in the heart of Whistler Village, but evergreens keep it hidden. Have a picnic here.

If biking, hiking, or walking isn't your thing, or if you just feel like spending a couple of hours floating, rent a canoe or kayak at one of the many outlets in Whistler Village. Lakeside Park on the shores of Alta Lake is one place to start. The **River of Golden Dreams** flows from Alta Lake and is a hands-down favorite among paddlers.

AFTERNOON

Squamish Lil'wat Cultural Centre, 4584 Blackcomb Way; (866) 441-7522; www.slcc.ca. Showcases Whistler's aboriginal heritage through Native art and interactive exhibits, both indoors and outside. The center, at the base of Blackfoot Mountain, features a museum and contemporary gallery, a great hall, museum, theater, restaurant, and gift shop. The spacious 3-story building rests on more than 4 acres of land and is surrounded by a hemlock grove. The design emulates a Squamish longhouse and a Lil'wat pit house. Large windows not only bring in plenty of light, but also show off spectacular mountains and old forests. The great hall features a new 40-foot-long canoe hand-carved from a single cedar log. The 80-seat theater shows a 15-minute film, *Where Rivers, Mountain and People Meet,* explaining both the historic and modern life of the First Nations people. Other exhibits include wool weavings, costumes, carvings, and other arts.

DINNER **Whistler Tasting Tours.** With some advance planning to make reservations, you can enjoy dining on a 4-course meal, where each course is provided by 4 different high-quality restaurants, and paired with a variety of British Columbia wines. For more information call (604) 902-8687 or view www.whistlertastingtours.com/contact. The tour is an excellent way to sample different restaurants when you are in Whistler for a short visit.

LODGING **Chalet Luise Bed & Breakfast Inn.**

DAY 3 / MORNING

BREAKFAST **Chalet Luise Bed & Breakfast Inn.**

After breakfast, make your way back to Seattle following the same Sea to Sky route, and consider stopping at some of the attractions you missed on the drive north. As you drive south, you will be able to complete your cultural history lessons of the region when you stop at kiosks 6 and 7.

There's More . . . .

Art galleries. Black Tusk Gallery, 101-4359 Main St.; (877) 905-5540; www.blacktusk.ca. Located in the Hilton Hotel, 108-4293 Mountain Square, is a First Nations gallery that exhibits Northwest Coast Native artists. Although collectors are the primary customers for the inventory in this high-end gallery, it's an opportunity for visitors at Whistler to see truly fine indigenous art.

Golf. Furry Creek Golf & Country Club, 150 Country Club Rd., Furry Creek; (888) 922-9462; www.furrycreekgolf.com. One of B.C.'s most scenic golf courses has everything: ocean, mountains, islands.

   Squamish Valley Golf Club, 2458 Mamquam Rd.; (888) 349-3688; www.squamishvalleygolf.com. Another picturesque course you won't forget.

Parks. Alice Lake Provincial Park, www.env.gov.bc.ca/bcparks/explore /parkpgs/alice_lk. Four freshwater lakes dominate this park-scape, making the spot a popular haven for families who love to camp or spend a day swimming. Two of the lakes have lovely sandy beaches and changing houses.

   Garibaldi Provincial Park, www.env.gov.bc.ca/bcparks/explore /parkpgs/garibaldi. Even in September, you should check the road conditions, as the snow sometimes arrives in very early fall. Dense forests hug gemlike azure lakes. Snowcapped jagged peaks frame the lakes year-round.

   Rainbow Park, in Whistler Valley. Rainbow Park on Alta Lake offers a soft, sandy beach and shallow waters that are perfect for young children when supervision is available. Picnic tables, barbecues, and a broad, grassy lawn with shade trees give families a reason to stay all afternoon.

Walking trails. **Brandywine Falls Trail,** north of Squamish. Take a short walk across the covered footbridge, through the forest, to a viewing platform overlooking the 230-foot Brandywine Falls. Another path takes you to a second viewpoint of the falls and the area surrounding Daisy Lake and the Black Tusk.

    Trail to Cal-Cheak Suspension Bridge. Allow 2 hours for your return. This trail travels through mixed Douglas fir and lodgepole pine forests among outcrops of lava beds and small ponds.

Special Events . . . .

MID-JUNE THROUGH MID-OCTOBER
Whistler Farmers' Market. Every Sunday. Fresh local produce and arts and crafts.

JULY 1 THROUGH AUGUST 31
Artwalk. More than 20 regional artists and artisans display their wares through Whistler Village.

LATE JULY
Canadian National BBQ Championships. Those who think they are familiar with barbecue flavors are always surprised when they attend this event, which draws competitors from around the country. For just $5, visitors can sample several entries, and see for themselves just how different barbecue recipes can be.

Other Recommended Restaurants and Lodging . . . .

BRACKENDALE

The Nest, 41340 Government Rd.; (604) 898-4444; www.thenest rest.com. Winner of several readers' choice awards, including best steak and best pasta. Open for dinner and brunch on weekends.

WHISTLER

Brio House, 3005 Brio Entrance; (604) 932-3313. On Sea to Sky Highway. Bed-and-breakfast with filling gourmet breakfasts, and an additional 3-bedroom mountain chalet year-round that sleeps up to 9 people. Free guest shuttle to and from Whistler gondola.

Cedar Springs Bed & Breakfast Lodge, 8106 Cedar Springs Rd.; (800) 727-7547 or (604) 938-8007; www.whistlerinns.com. Eight lodge rooms. Sunken hot tub. Great room with home theater TV and DVD player. Homemade cookies and hot chocolate.

Crepe-Montagne, 116-4368 Main St. (tucked away behind the Market Place IGA); (604) 905-4444; www.crepemontagne.com. Breakfast menu offers eggs Benedict, bacon, eggs, pancakes, Belgian waffles, and savory or sweet crepes. Large selection of savory crepes for both lunch and dinner.

Durlacher Hof, 7055 Nesters Rd.; (604) 932-1924; www.durlacher hof.com. A variety of rooms and suites, furnished with attractive and sturdy pine furnishings. Its chalet-style restaurant serves Austrian raisin pancakes as part of its full complimentary breakfast. Close walk to Whistler Village.

Inn at Clifftop Lane Bed & Breakfast, 2828 Clifftop Lane; (604) 938-1229 or (888) 281-2929; www.innatclifftop.com. Whistler's highest rated B&B, located in a quiet Whistler neighborhood. Holds title in "the best places to kiss in the Northwest" category. Attractive interior painting and furnishing. Covered hot tub on patio. TV, cable, and DVD/VCR in every room. Full complimentary breakfast with fruits, breads, pastries, and a hot entree.

Sundial Boutique Hotel, 4340 Sundial Crescent; (877) 570-1187; www.sundialhotel.com. European-style lodging with many amenities for couples, families, and groups, including 3 on-site restaurants and a coin-operated laundry. Attractive rooms, and 1- and 2-bedroom suites, some with mountain views. Modern furnishings in soothing tones.

For More Information . . . .

BC Parks, www.env.gov.bc.ca/bcparks. Lists all parks and their amenities, provides camping reservation information, and highlights activities for each park.

BC Passport, www.bcpassport.com/default.aspx. Information about train transportation between Vancouver and Whistler.

Hello B.C., www.hellobc.com. Tourism British Columbia website that provides up-to-date information on hotels, transportation, and activities throughout the province.

Whistler Blackcomb Office, 4545 Blackcomb Way; (866) 218-9690; www.whistlerblackcomb.com.

NORTHBOUND ESCAPE *Five*
Whidbey Island to Bellingham
MEANDERING THROUGH PARKS, GARDENS,
AND FARMS / 1 NIGHT

Art galleries
Deception Pass State Park
Ferry rides
Old forts
Panoramic views
Scenic Chuckanut Drive

You might not have ventured to Whidbey Island before, because it seemed too much like exploring your own backyard. However, Whidbey Island, considered the longest island in the continental United States, has a lot of variety tucked away in a relatively small space.

One of the best things about Whidbey are the views at almost every turn, because it is surrounded by Puget Sound. Just about everywhere you go, you will have majestic views of either the Olympic or Cascade mountains or Mount Baker and Mount Rainier, whether on a ferry boat, a harbor, or a windswept beach, or in one of the tiny towns that line SR 20.

No visitor should miss an opportunity to attend a county fair and a farmers' market on the island. These open-air events invariably convene folks who love nothing more than a friendly conversation about life on the island.

As you leave Whidbey Island from the north, some of the most dramatic scenery in the state awaits you at Deception Pass Bridge. Not as dramatic but undeniably beautiful is the back road you will take from Anacortes to Bellingham.

You begin your next escape on a ferry boat. After driving I-5 north to Mukilteo on SR 525, board the Mukilteo ferry. Debark from the ferry at the town of Clinton on Whidbey Island. Take SR 525 to Freeland. After approximately 25 miles, SR 525

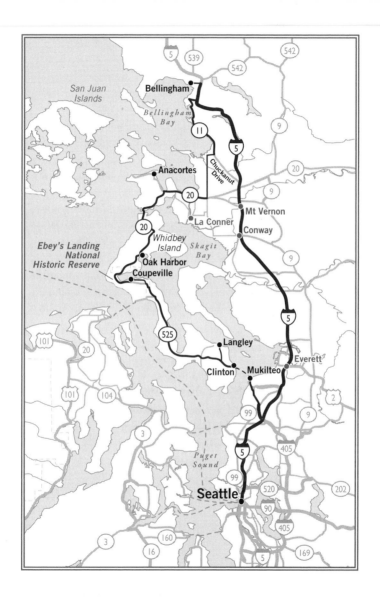

becomes SR 20, which runs to the northern boundary of Whidbey Island.

DAY 1 / MORNING

Clinton is the first town you pass through. The award-winning **Clinton Beach Park** is a driftwood beach where you will also find original artwork and a playground.

The seaside village of **Langley,** northwest of Clinton, has several galleries (Brackenwood Gallery, Callahan's Firehouse Studio and Gallery), antiques shops (Virginia's Antiques, Whidbey Island Antiques), and bookstores (Gregor Rare Books, Moonraker Bookstore, and South Whidbey Commons Coffeehouse Bookstore).

Freeland is a town on one of the narrowest parts of the island that started in 1900 as an experiment in socialism, in which the local land was to be free to all the residents. Today the community is best known as a home to many of the island's artists, who find a constant source of inspiration in the nearby wildlife, beaches, and tide pools.

Just north is the horticulturalist's haven, **Greenbank Farm,** located on the fringes of **Greenbank.** Ste. Michelle Winery owned the 522-acre farm until 1996, when it listed the property for sale. Concerned about a lack of say about how the property would be developed, a consortium of the Island County, the Port of Coupeville, and the Nature Conservancy purchased the property. Also inside the garden is **Meerkerk Rhododendron Gardens** (www.meerkerkgardens .org), with 10 acres of display and educational gardens tucked away in a woodland preserve with easy walking trails open to the public. On the farm are the original 1904 barn, a gift shop, and a tasting room for sampling Washington wines. Greenbank Farm is now the setting for festivals, farmers' markets, and the Highland Games, an authentic Scottish celebration complete with bagpipes and drums, Celtic harp competitions, and a *ceilidh,* a traditional Scottish party on Saturday evening.

Continuing north, **Fort Casey State Park** (www.parks.wa.gov/parks /?selectedpark=Fort%20Casey) is a 467-acre marine camping park with 35 sites. Visitors can view Admiralty Head Lighthouse and climb around the emplacements to see the bunkers that were provided for soldiers. As is true throughout the island, the views of the Olympics and Admiralty Inlet are splendid.

Close by is **San de Fuca,** a small town from the late 1800s and early 1900s. It's still on the maps, but all that remains is the 1902 school building, overlooking Penn Cove. West of Penn Cove is **Fort Ebey State Park,** a 645-mile camping park that was originally built as a coastal defense fort during World War II. Concrete platforms mark the previous gun turrets. The park has 3 miles of saltwater shoreline on the Strait of Juan de Fuca, a freshwater lake for fishing, and miles of hiking and biking trails. To reach the park, turn west on Libbey Road and follow it 1½ miles to Hill Valley Drive. Turn left and enter the park. More information is available at www.parks.wa.gov/parks/?selectedpark=Fort%20 Ebey. **Coupeville,** one of Washington's oldest towns, was founded in 1852, originally as a small port. Remnants of times gone by are still in full view at the old Coupeville wharf building, originally built in 1905 to store locally grown grain and provide ferry services. These days there's a crowded souvenir shop that carries a great selection of postcards and maps of the region. You can buy gifts to take home at **Local Grown,** 26 Front St. (360-678-3648; www.whidbeylocalgrown.org), adjacent to the souvenir shop. The store sells a nice variety of locally produced wines, honeys, and jams. Across the hall is Kim's Cafe, where you will have lunch.

LUNCH   **Kim's Cafe,** 26 Front St.; (360) 678-4924. Suitable for kids, who like to order grilled cheese sandwiches and corn dogs. But Kim's, owned and operated by a local family, mainly serves tasty and authentic Thai and Vietnamese food inside its large cafe, and outdoors on the deck, too. The best part of dining at Kim's is the incredible view of Mount Baker and the closer boat activity around Penn Cove.

Front Street is lined with quality shops: Touch of Dutch, selling Dutch imports, the Honey Bear, a toy and candy shop, and Tea and Talk, selling tea and accessories and English treats.

At the end of the block is **Island County Historical Museum,** 908 NW Alexander St. (360-678-3310; www.islandhistory.org), worth stopping at to browse the exhibits about the Native American culture and the seafaring pioneers.

DINNER   **Front Street Grill,** 20 NW Front St., (360) 682-2551; www .frontstreetgrillcoupeville.com. For seafood lovers, a wide array of entrees that will please: cioppino, mussels, oysters, prawns, and ahi tuna. Vegetarian and meat entrees complete this tasty menu.

LODGING   **Anchorage Inn Bed & Breakfast,** 807 North Main St.; (877) 230-1313 or (360) 678-5581; www.anchorage-inn.com. Seven pretty rooms offer views of the cove, or the waterfronts or Mount Baker. Next door the 2-bedroom Calista Cottage vacation rental is a historic house built in 1883. Just a few steps away are storefront shops and restaurants.

DAY 2 / MORNING

BREAKFAST   **Anchorage Inn Bed & Breakfast** serves a full breakfast with fresh fruit, juice, breads, and a breakfast entree.

Oak Harbor is home to the **Whidbey Island Naval Air Station,** which provides economic stability to the area. The station employs 10,000 active-duty personnel, civilians, and contractors. Naturally, the population supports a large number of big-box discount stores and chain fast-food restaurants, but the waterfront street remains charming and has its share of interesting shops.

Farther north, take some time at **Deception Pass.** Walk along the bridge on either side of the highway. Take a walk along one of the forested trails off to the side. Snap photos. But mainly, take a deep breath and be in awe of the forces of nature (the pass) and the genius of humankind (the bridge).

Drive to **Anacortes,** a small town that frequently makes it onto lists for "best art towns." Wander by foot and see more than 100 murals that will nudge you to consider stories of times past. The city has a brochure, the *Walking Tour of Historic Downtown Anacortes,* which provides a fine activity before you leave. Take SR 20 to **Chuckanut Drive** (SR 11). The winding, scenic road provides 20 fabulous miles of scenic views of Padilla and Samish bays and the San Juan Islands, before it skirts Larrabee State Park and enters the historic district of Fairhaven in south Bellingham.

Before leaving for home, have a scone and cup of tea at the **Abbey Garden Tea Room,** 1312 11th St. (360-752-1752; www .abbeygardentea.com).

Leave Bellingham by turning right at Broadway and continue onto Sunset Drive, then turn left and merge onto I-5 south.

There's More . . . .

ANACORTES
Museums. **Anacortes History Museum,** 1305 8th St.; (360) 293-1915; http://museum.cityofanacortes.org. A former Carnegie

Library that maintains a permanent display and has revolving exhibits of the region's history.

COUPEVILLE
Farms. **Lavender Wind Farm,** 2530 Darst Rd.; (360) 678-0919 or (877) 242-7716; www.lavenderwind.com. Located on the west side of the island, this organic lavender farm offers inspiration in gardens with 9,000 lavender plants and a meditative labyrinth. A well-stocked gift shop sells several types of lavender in bulk, as well as culinary lavender, lavender bathing and hair products, and every other lavender product you can imagine.

PENN COVE
Shopping. **Penn Cove Pottery,** SR 20, at the 26-mile marker between Coupeville and Oak Harbor; (360) 678-6464; www.penncovegallery .com. Quilts, glass, and pottery by local artists.

Other Recommended Restaurants and Lodging . . . .

ANACORTES
Anaco Bay Inn, 916 33rd St.; (360) 299-3320; www.anacobayinn .com. A European-style inn. Some rooms have hot tubs, kitchens. Continental breakfast.

Gere-a-Deli, 502 Commercial Ave.; (360) 293-8042. A retro-style eatery with high ceilings and plenty of old signage on the walls to entertain while you wait for fresh-made sandwiches, chowder, or an old-fashioned dessert.

CLINTON
The Farmhouse Bed & Breakfast, 2740 E. Sunshine Lane; (360) 321-6288 or (888) 888-7022; www.farmhousebb.com. Offers 4

garden-themed suites and views of Useless Bay, Sunlight Beach, and Puget Sound. Breakfast is served in the privacy of your room.

COUPEVILLE
The Blue Goose Inn, 702 N. Main St.; (360) 678-4284 or (877) 678-4284; www.bluegooseinn.com. Actually 2 Victorian-style homes, with 4 large suites and 2 bedrooms. Soft colors and tasteful antiques. Satisfying breakfasts.

GREENBANK
Whidbey Pies, Cafe & Catering, 765 Wonn Rd.; (360) 678-1288; www.whidbeypies.com. Famous for its loganberry pies, chock-full of the berries that made Greenbank Farms famous.

LANGLEY
Inn at Langley, 400 1st St.; (360) 221-3033; www.innatlangley .com/about. Has won awards from *Travel & Leisure, Condé Nast Traveler, National Geographic Traveler,* and *Sunset* magazines. Sixteen guest rooms with views of the Saratoga Passage, 2 master suites, and 2 cottages. All beautifully designed and exceedingly well furnished. Complimentary breakfast of scones, yogurt, fruit.

Saratoga Inn, 201 Cascade Ave.; (360) 221-5801 or (866) 749-5565; www.saratogainnwhidbeyisland.com. Views of the Saratoga Passage and the North Cascades. Full breakfast, afternoon tea, wine and hors d'oeuvres in the afternoon, fresh-baked cookies and desserts. Accommodation choices include a carriage house, and king and queen guest rooms.

OAK HARBOR
Seabolt's Smokehouse, 31640 SR 20, Suite 3; (360) 675-6485; www.seabolts.com. Small and casual; open every day. Not

inexpensive, but diners rave about the freshest ever fish and chips here. Salmon pâté and smoked salmon are other popular items.

Special Events . . . .

MARCH

Penn Cove's Coupeville Mussel Festival. A 2-day event in honor of the region's renowned flavorful mussel, which attaches itself naturally to the rocks and the wharf pilings in the cove. Visitors have the chance to sample the freshest mussels, presented in a variety of mouth-watering ways.

AUGUST

Coupeville Arts and Crafts Festival. Two-day street fair with quality arts and entertainment.

Anacortes Arts Festival. For more than 50 years, the community of Anacortes has been celebrating its arts community with this 3-day event of food—from kebabs and curry to fruit smoothies and salmon—and 260 artisans representing almost every medium, from metal sculpture to basketry.

SEPTEMBER

Whidbey Island Farm Tours. More than 2 dozen of the island's farms open their gates for the general public to visit. These self-guided tours of local working farms offer islanders and tourists alike the chance to learn about the daily operations, and respective challenges, in running a farm.

OCTOBER

Greenbank Farm Oktoberfest. This is a fund-raiser that features a 10-piece oompah band, bratwurst, and beer gardens, as well as face painting for the children and a costume contest for dogs.

For More Information . . . .

Bellingham/Whatcom Chamber of Commerce & Industry, P.O. Box 958, Bellingham, WA 98227; (360) 734-1330; www.bellingham .com.

Central Whidbey Chamber & Visitor Information, 23 NW Front St., Coupeville, WA 98239; (360) 678-5434; www.centralwhidbey chamber.com/index.html.

Chamber of Commerce Anacortes, 819 Commercial Ave., Suite F, Anacortes, WA 98221; (360) 293-7911; www.anacortes.org.

Clinton Chamber of Commerce, P.O. Box 444, Clinton, WA 98236; (360) 341-3929.

Greater Oak Harbor Chamber of Commerce, 32630 SR 20, Oak Harbor, WA 98277; (360) 675-3755; http://oakharborchamber .com.

Langley Chamber of Commerce, 208 Anthes Ave., Langley, WA 98260; (360) 221-6765; www.visitlangley.com.

Washington State Ferries, 2901 3rd Ave., Suite 500, Seattle; (888) 808-7977; www.wsdot.wa.gov/ferries.

EASTBOUND *ESCAPES*

EASTBOUND ESCAPE *One*

Hells Canyon

SNAKING THROUGH HELLS CANYON NATIONAL
RECREATION AREA / 2 NIGHTS

- Mile-deep canyon
- Petroglyphs
- Wilderness lodge
- Mail boats
- Whitewater rafting
- Jet boating

A vacation along the Snake River in Lewiston, Idaho, near Hells Canyon National Recreation Area, remains a perennial favorite among northwesterners who crave outdoor adventure. Located in a pleasant lowland valley at just 736 feet above sea level, there's easy access from Lewiston to both the valleys in the west and to the canyons in the south. The mighty Snake cuts through the high desert plateaus of Washington and Oregon, and the craggy mountains of Idaho, before plunging between the narrow walls of Hells Canyon. Native Americans took refuge here. Miners, ranchers, and steamboaters all have tried to tame the canyon, but only a few stubborn ranchers have survived and managed to become permanent residents.

Hells Canyon is paradise for birders. Songbirds of all kinds, and many species of owls, hawks, eagles, falcons, and waterfowl, make their homes here—at least part of the year. But elk, mule deer, Rocky Mountain bighorn sheep, mountain goats, black bears, cougars, and coyotes are among the other wildlife that visitors can spot with the naked eye or binoculars. Outfitters and guides lead hikes for wildlife spotting as well as to abandoned pioneer cabins, mines, and other Native American historic sites.

Lewiston is located in northwestern Idaho, on the border with Washington. The original capital of Idaho Territory, Lewiston holds a great deal of history. Explorers Lewis and Clark camped in this area

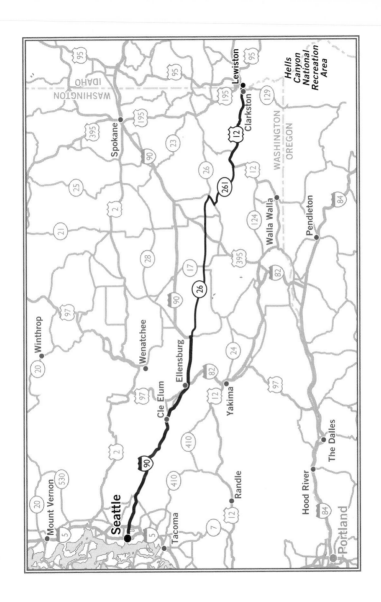

on their epic voyage westward, donating their names to Lewiston and to the adjacent town of Clarkston, Washington.

While the state of Washington between Seattle and Lewiston is vast, diverse, and frequently spectacular—and therefore worth driving—a flight from Seattle to Lewiston takes just 32 minutes and costs only $200. Check Booking Buddy (www.bookingbuddy .com) or one of your favorite search engines, such as Expedia (www .expedia.com), for flights. If you have more time, driving is obviously another option to consider. If you do drive, you might incorporate Eastbound Escape Four through Leavenworth to Yakima.

The drive from Seattle to Lewiston is 265 miles and takes about 6 hours. Take I-5 south, then merge onto I-90 east. Follow signs from Seattle to Bellevue on I-90, then merge onto SR 26 toward Othello-Pullman. Take SR 260 to SR 261 south. Then take US 12 east to Lewiston.

The options for this escape are many. Take your pick!

DAY 1 / MORNING

Depart for **Lewiston** via Sea-Tac Airport. Plan to arrive by late morning so you can enjoy Lewiston and prepare for a Hells Canyon overnight boat trip. Pick up a self-guided historic walking tour map at the Lewiston Chamber office. Take some time to view the numerous pieces of public art, such as the modern bronze fountain depicting three children playing in the pool of water, located at **Brackenbury Square** on Lewiston's Main Street, or the bronze sculpture of longtime local newspaper reporter, Tom Campbell, in **Tribune Plaza.** A bronze sculpture of a Nez Perce warrior on an Appaloosa horse, titled *Indian Summer 1974,* is located at the **Nez Perce County courthouse.** Lewiston's **Historic Shopping District** provides visitors the opportunity to step back to a time when shopping took place at a leisurely pace. The tree-lined Main Street is home to several shops selling antiques, artwork, jewelry, clothing, gifts, and furniture. For more information, see www .beautifuldowntownlewiston.com.

LUNCH   **Zany's Hollywood Grill,** 2004 19th Ave.; (208) 746-8131. A '50s-style grill with Hollywood memorabilia. Good service and gourmet burgers served with fries or slaw.

AFTERNOON

Visit the **Lewis & Clark Center for Arts and History,** 415 Main St. (208-792-2243; www.go-idaho.com/Lewis-Clark-Center-for-Arts-and-History), which displays local and Nez Perce art, and artifacts of Chinese immigrants who lived in the region. Believe it or not, Idaho does have a port, and it's in Lewiston. Close to the port is the **Nez Perce County Historical Society Inc. & Museum,** 0306 3rd St. (208-743-2535; www.npchistsoc.org). This small museum contains fine exhibits and materials on the Nez Perce tribes as well as the Lewis and Clark Expedition of Discovery. Relax and watch the boat traffic from the dock before dinner.

DINNER   **Macullen's Steak, Seafood & Spirit House,** 1516 Main St.; (208) 746-3438; www.macullens.com. You can fill up on plates of appetizers such as giant chilled prawns and fried ravioli, but you might want to save room for one of the several steak entrees or perhaps Greek chicken or a panko-crusted halibut.

LODGING   **Guesthouse Inn & Suites,** 1325 Main St.; (800) 214-8378 or (208) 746-3311; www.guesthouseintl.com/Home. A 75-room facility with standard accommodations at a reasonable price, and an extended continental breakfast. Wi-Fi available.

DAY 2 / MORNING

....

BREAKFAST   Extended continental breakfast at **Guesthouse Inn & Suites.**

Take full advantage of the canyon's wonders in a relatively short period of time by purchasing a package with one of the several licensed outfitters, such as **Beamer's Hells Canyon Tours,** 1451 Bridge St., Clarkston (800-522-6966 or 509-758-4800; www .hellscanyontours.com), the largest of several riverboat companies. There's something for everyone—the young and the old, the adventuresome and those who simply wish to soak up Mother Nature. Outings are available for all levels of experience, to ensure that each journey over the riffles and rapids of the Snake River and through Hells Canyon—the deepest canyon in North America—is both pleasant and safe.

No matter which overnight trip you choose, make sure you dress warmly and comfortably, with shoes appropriate for riverside docks, water, and rustic pathways. Plan to get a little river water on your face when opening and closing the sliding glass jet-boat windows for a better view or paddling your raft.

On Beamer's popular jet-boat tours, which run daily May through September and cover just under 200 miles round-trip, you'll pass like a bucking bronco over raging rapids into the deepest river gorge in North America. (The rides are gentler in the summer and fall.)

A US Coast Guard–certified tour captain covers topics ranging from Native American history, geology, and the history of sternwheelers to cattle ranching and US Mail services. He stops at some of the more significant historical points. Scattered throughout the canyon are a wealth of archaeological sites, such as pit house villages and rock shelters. Also protected here are Native American petroglyphs and pictographs etched and painted onto rock faces. Approximately 90 minutes after your tour departs, you will stop at a coffee and juice bar. Help yourself to fresh-baked muffins and fruit, served in the comfort of the climate-controlled riverfront Heller Bar Lodge.

LUNCH Your box lunch, served at **Copper Creek Lodge** (800-522-6966; www.hellscanyontours.com), includes an overstuffed deli sandwich with condiments, potato chips and granola bar, iced tea, and lemonade.

AFTERNOON

You will visit the **Kirkwood Historic Ranch** and log museum, accessible only by boat or trail, and maintained by the US Forest Service. The museum, once a bunkhouse for ranch hands, features exhibits that help visitors picture what canyon life was like in the 1930s. Also on display are arrowheads and fossils. The ranch is located on a narrow, flat bank that frames the river. The land was either farmed or ranched from the mid-1800s to 1974, when the government created the recreation area. Besides the museum are several outbuildings and a large collection of historic farming equipment. Most visitors take advantage of the walking tour at the onetime homestead of Len Jordan, who later became governor of Idaho and a US senator. His wife, Grace, wrote *Home Below Hells Canyon,* describing her family's years at Kirkwood Ranch.

DINNER **Copper Creek Lodge.** You will return 70 miles upriver in the wilds of Hells Canyon, where you eat a hearty meal around large tables in the dining hall. All-you-can-eat home-style meals at the main lodge leave everyone satisfied.

LODGING **Copper Creek Lodge.** Rustic yet containing the comforts of home, including bed and bath linens, and a hot shower.

DAY 3 / MORNING

....

BREAKFAST **Copper Creek Lodge** serves an old-fashioned rancher's breakfast.

If you flew, you have probably reserved a late-afternoon flight out of Lewiston Airport.

Some visitors plan their escape to hop on one of Beamer's popular 200-mile round-trip mail boat tours, which leave every Wednesday at 9 a.m. This is a 2-day, 1-night adventure. One- to 3-day fishing boat charters are also available, as are whitewater rafting trips along the Snake River, renowned for its plummeting whitewater, and with names such as Wild Sheep, Granite, Waterspout, and Rush Creek rapids. Other packages include hiking and camping in gorgeous, remote canyon areas, with outfitters packing the gear on horses or llamas. On fully outfitted trips, guides provide all the food and camping equipment. Spring and fall are recommended for these tours, when crowds are few and temperatures moderate. See a map at www.hellscanyontours.com/pdfs/HellsCanyonMap.pdf.

There's More . . . .

Farmers' markets. D Street parking lot, Lewiston; (208) 746-6246; www .localharvest.org. Fresh local produce, meat, poultry, eggs, gifts, flowers, bread, pastries, and coffee. Live music on Wed June through Sept.

Parks. **Chief Looking Glass Park,** 5 miles south of Clarkston on SR 129 on lower Granite Lake; (509) 751-0240. Offers boat launch ramps to the Snake River, as well as docks, moorage, and picnic tables. From there you can follow the 16-mile wheelchair-accessible Clearwater and Snake River National Recreation Trail to historic sites and attractions in Hells Gate State Park, Swallows Nest Rock, and West Pond.

Chief Timothy State Park, 8 miles west of Clarkston off US 12, sits on an island in the middle of the Snake River; (208) 743-6855. The Alpowai Interpretive Center offers audiovisual programs and exhibits.

Hells Gate State Park, Lewiston. Soak up Lewis and Clark country from this grassy, shaded campground along the shores of the Snake River. Insider tip: Hike an easy 1½ miles south to a 150-foot-tall ancient lava formation.

Lewis and Clark National Historical Tour, near Highway 12 between Lolo Pass and Lewiston; (208) 926-4274.

Whitewater rafting. **Barker River Trips,** 2124 Grelle Ave., Lewiston; (208) 743-7459 or (800) 353-7459; www.barker-river-trips .com. Guided river trips on Salmon, Grande Ronde, Cotahuasi, and Owyhee Rivers. Oar and paddle rafts, inflatable kayaks, and dory drift boats. May through Sept.

Hells Canyon Adventures, P.O. Box 159, Oxbow, OR 97840; (541) 785-3352 or (800) 422-3568; www.hellscanyonadventures .com. Offers whitewater rafting as well as day or overnight jet-boat tours.

ROW Adventures, 2332 Florence Lane, Clarkston; (800) 451-6034; www.rowadventures.com. ROW offers whitewater rafting on the Salmon and Snake Rivers of Hells Canyon for families and groups.

Snake Dancer Excursions, (800) 234-1941; www.snakedancer excursions.com. May be the best bet for those wanting a half-day jet-boat tour of Hells Canyon. The tour on the company's small boat lasts about 5½ hours, which might be sufficient for families with small children or for people who just want a sample of the Hells Canyon.

Wineries. **Clearwater Canyon Cellars,** 1708 6th Ave. N, Suite A, Lewiston; (208) 746-7975; www.clearwatercanyoncellars.com.

This is Lewiston's first commercial winery since Prohibition. Premium wines from Northwest grapes, crafted by local artisans.

Special Events . . . .

APRIL

Dogwood Festival, Lewiston. Thirty-day event that includes garden tours and crafts fair.

LATE APRIL

Asotin County Fair, Clarkston. Features rodeo, stock show, and sale.

JUNE

I Made the Grade Bicycle Race, Clarkston. Thirteen-mile bicycle ride that climbs 1,000 feet.

LATE JUNE

Lewis and Clark Discovery Faire, Lewiston. Commemorates the Lewis and Clark Corps of Discovery with food, entertainment, and arts and crafts vendors.

SEPTEMBER

Nez Perce County Fair, Lewiston. Includes agricultural, livestock, and homemaking competitions, carnival and midway, and commercial booths.

Lewiston Roundup, Lewiston. One of the largest professional rodeos in the Pacific Northwest.

MID-DECEMBER

Christmas Reflections on the Confluence, Clarkston. Lighted boat parade on the Snake River near Swallows Nest Park.

Other Recommended Restaurants and Lodging . . . .

CLARKSTON, WASHINGTON

Cliff House Bed & Breakfast, 1227 Westlake Dr.; (509) 758-1267; www.cliffhouseclarkston.com. Perched on a hillside with outstanding views of the Snake River. An intimate setting with just 2 guest rooms. Deck offers opportunities for viewing hawks, eagles, and osprey, and enjoying a full breakfast.

Fazzari's, 1281 Bridge St.; (509) 758-3386; www.fazzaris.com. Customers can watch the chefs tossing the dough that transforms into superthin, tender crust for traditional and designer pizzas. They also serve baked pasta dishes and offer a small selection of sandwiches and salads.

LEWISTON, IDAHO

Inn America, 702 21st St.; (208) 746-4600 or (800) 469-4667; www.innamerica.com. Travelers consider this simple hotel, which overlooks the river, a good value. Continental breakfast is included.

Italianna Inn, 2728 11th Ave.; (877) 550-2662; www.italiannainn .com. The inn's Italian-born landlady makes sure you have everything you need to be comfortable. Much like a luxury accommodation in the Tuscany countryside, here a gracious patio surrounds a swimming pool, and a lovely vineyard envelops the villa.

Mandarin Pine Restaurant, 833 21st St.; (208) 746-4919; www .mandarinpine.com. Open every day for lunch and dinner, this restaurant serves traditional chow mein and stir-fried rice, plus a good selection of chicken, beef, and shrimp entrees. A children's menu includes burgers and sandwiches.

Thai Taste Restaurant, 1410 21st St.; (208) 746-6192. Fresh ingredients prepared on the spot. Wonton, egg rolls, and fried rice are popular choices. Vegetarian options, too.

For More Information . . . .

Clarkston Chamber of Commerce, 502 Bridge St., Clarkston, WA 99403; (509) 758-7712 or (800) 993-2128; www.clarkston chamber.org and www.visitclarkston.com/OnlineGuide.html.

Hells Canyon Visitors Association, 504 Bridge St., Clarkston, WA 99403; (509) 758-7489 or (877) 774-7248; www.hellscanyon visitor.com.

Idaho Outfitters & Guides Association, P.O. Box 95, Boise, ID 83701; (800) 49-IDAHO or (208) 342-1438; www.ioga.org.

Lewiston Chamber of Commerce, 111 Main St., No. 120, Lewiston, ID 83501; (208) 743-3531 or (800) 473-3543; www.lewiston chamber.org.

Lewiston–Nez Perce County Regional Airport, www.lcairport.net. Alaska Airlines (800-252-7522), Horizon Air (800-547-9308), and SkyWest (through United Express, 800-864-8331) offer frequent direct flights to and from Seattle.

Booking Buddy, www.bookingbuddy.com. Online reservation service for travel and hotel reservations and car rentals.

Expedia, www.expedia.com; (800) 551-2409. Online reservation service for travel and hotel reservations and car rentals.

EASTBOUND ESCAPE *Two*

Snoqualmie Valley

VISITING THE WATERFALLS OF THE MOON PEOPLE /
1 NIGHT

Long before the explorers and hop growers reached Snoqualmie Valley, Native American tribes met for trade and council beside the thundering torrent now called Snoqualmie Falls. Early settlers referred to the Natives who lived along the riverbanks as the "moon people," for their name was said to be derived from Snoqualm, meaning "moon."

> Dramatic waterfall
> Hiking trails
> Historical museums
> Medieval village
> Regional wildlife park
> Steam train ride

The first white settlers arrived in 1855. By the early 20th century, hops, timber, and electrical power that harnessed the falls' tremendous energy were important segments of the local economy. Today it's tourism. Just 20 miles from Seattle, the charming little burgs of Preston, Fall City, Carnation, Snoqualmie, and North Bend all offer a slower pace to visitors who stroll down their cheerful Main Streets.

The scenic valley is webbed with quiet back roads that pass farmlands, forests, mountains, and gurgling streams on their way to the Snoqualmie River. This getaway offers a chance to both refresh the spirit and choose from a variety of recreational activities.

DAY 1 / MORNING

Travel on I-90 east from Seattle to exit 27, a 30-minute drive. Follow the signs to Snoqualmie. Plan to arrive about 10 a.m. so that

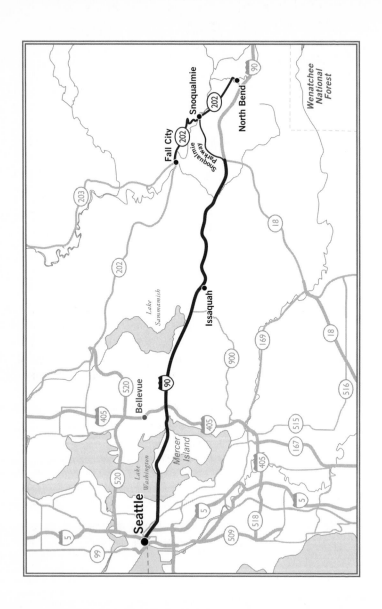

you'll have an hour to explore the little town and its quaint, restored train depot and **Northwest Railway Museum,** 38625 SE King St., before your train ride. Built in 1890, the depot is on the National Register of Historic Places. Its displays include a sizable collection of rolling stock from steam, electric, and logging railroads. The museum is open daily from 10 a.m. to 5 p.m.

Now board the old-fashioned steam- or diesel-powered train for a 10-mile trip through the scenic valley. The vintage coaches pass by the base of rugged Mount Si and the top of Snoqualmie Falls, and through dense forests. They clickety-clack over bridges and through lush green fields to a scenic viewing point before making the return trip to the Snoqualmie depot.

Trains run July through October. Fares are $12 for adults, $10 for seniors over 62, and $8 for children 3 to 12. The ride takes 70 minutes. For schedule information, call (425) 888-3030 or view www.trainmuseum.org/Trains.asp.

LUNCH **Woodman Lodge Steakhouse & Saloon,** 38601 SE King St.; (425) 888-4441. Located ½ block from the railroad museum, the restaurant building originally belonged to the Woodman Camp 8630, a fraternal organization serving coal miners, lumberjacks, and railroad workers. The interior, with pressed-tin ceilings and Douglas fir floors, has been beautifully restored. The long, wood-framed bar with a sparkling clean mirror behind it is a popular seating area for folks who come out just for the toothsome appetizers. Pomegranate spinach, Caesar, and steak salads, as well as soups, flatbread sandwiches, and buffalo burgers topped with smoked gouda and served with hand-cut fries, all make good lunch choices. After you finish, ask your waiter if you can go upstairs to see the restored western ballroom. There's history everywhere you look in this vast old space. After lunch, head over to **Chew Chew Cafe and Candy,** 8102 Railroad Ave. SE (425-292-9516; www.facebook.com/pages/Chew-Chew-Cafe-and-Candy/155845911125657), for a scoop of ice cream, or a bag of nut brittles or caramel corn for the road. All are made on the premises.

AFTERNOON

....

After lunch, continue east on 384th Avenue to the freeway on-ramp and Winery Road, which you will follow to the 9-acre city-owned **Snoqualmie Point Park,** 37580 SE Winery Rd. This is no ordinary park, but one that will richly reward you with a panoramic view of the Snoqualmie Valley, Cascade Mountain Range, Mount Si, and Mount Baker. If you have a picnic lunch, sit under the shelter with its sweeping curved roof, supported by tree-trunk columns. The playful restroom is designed to look like the outhouse sheds commonly used in the early 20th century for logging operations. An 11-mile hiking trail starts next to the park and ends at Rattlesnake Lake, south of North Bend.

Now turn back toward Snoqualmie and follow the signs to Snoqualmie Falls, which are 1 mile from town. Fenced, paved paths along the cliff offer viewing points for watching the hurling cascade that obscures human chatter with its mighty roar. One hundred feet higher than Niagara Falls, the falls crash onto a misty pool down below.

To get closer to the falls, walk the ½-mile trail that descends to a rocky beach at the falls' base. Behind the powerhouse that stands above the beach, you'll find a plank walk leading to an elevated overlook that provides unobstructed views.

The trails and landscaped park on the cliff near the lodge were developed by Puget Power, which has received awards recognizing the park's design.

DINNER **Fall City Roadhouse and Inn.** Enjoy a home-cooked meal with foods that are grown and raised locally. You will retire upstairs for the night.

LODGING **Fall City Roadhouse and Inn,** 4200 Preston–Fall City Rd. SE; (425) 222-4040. Thoughtfully restored in 2008, the building once was a tavern, then in 1916, a lodging establishment called the Colonial Inn. The inn's exterior was the image used on the set of the award-winning TV series *Twin Peaks*. The rooms upstairs overlook Fall City and the Snoqualmie River. All have HD flat-screen TVs and the contemporary works of local artists. Most rooms have private bathrooms. The shared European-style showers in others means a great price for anyone on a tight budget.

DAY 2 / MORNING

Drive 20 miles south on SR 202 to North Bend. Turn left at the traffic signal, and continue to Mount Si Road. Take this road across the Snoqualmie River and park at a gravel area near the bridge. Walk a few yards on 432nd Avenue to the trailhead for **Little Mount Si.** The 2-mile trail is framed with forest all the way to the 1,000-foot summit. The views of the valley, Mount Si, and the Cascade Range in the distance are extraordinary.

Another 4-mile hike up the 4,190-foot-high **Mount Si** itself is more challenging. But the panoramic summit view makes Mount Si the second-most-hiked mountain in the state.

If you are not interested in hiking, you can visit the **Snoqualmie Valley Historical Museum,** 320 Bendigo Ave. S (425-888-3200; www.snoqualmievalleymuseum.org). In this former private home, volunteers maintain exhibits of regional pioneer memorabilia.

AFTERNOON

Take I-90 west to exit 17 and leave the freeway for **Issaquah,** a pretty village that is undergoing a growth spurt as urbanites move here from the greater Seattle area. Located adjacent to Issaquah's downtown district is the **Issaquah Salmon Hatchery,** 125 W. Sunset Way (www.issaquahfish.org), home to a well-preserved WPA-built structure, 19 rearing ponds, and 3 holding ponds. September and

October are the best months to visit, when the salmon return to the hatchery up Issaquah Creek. The Edelweiss Chalet on Gilman Boulevard is the headquarters for the renowned **Boehm's Candies**. Stop by for luscious hand-dipped chocolates at 55 NE Gilman Blvd. (425-392-6652; www.boehmscandies.com/catalog).

Drive north on Gilman and you'll find **Gilman Village,** a complex of fifty-odd shops and restaurants, many of them in old homes that were moved to the site by the Mohl family, who were passionate about saving the old, unwanted buildings scattered around the old farming and mining town of Issaquah. The Mohls' vision of renovating the structures and moving them together in a parklike setting to create an attractive retail haven has proved a boon for local independent shop owners.

A short distance past Gilman Village is **Gilman Antique Gallery,** 625 NW Gilman Blvd. (425-391-6640), a must for antiques' lovers. Here 170 exhibitors display thousands of antiques of all kinds.

Cougar Mountain Regional Wildlife Park, 19525 SE 54th St. (425-392-6278), is a 5-acre facility that provides a home for almost 300 threatened or endangered animal species. Open daily year-round for prearranged tours.

If you'd like a stroll on a sandy beach before you complete this escape, stop at **Lake Sammamish,** northwest of Issaquah off I-90. By then, plenty relaxed, you probably won't mind driving the last few miles into Seattle.

There's More . . . .

CARNATION
Farms. **Remlinger Farms,** 32610 NE 32nd St.; (425) 333-4135; www.remlingerfarms.com. Family-operated farm that's fun for all ages, with barnyard animals, a bakery and restaurant, and lots of fresh produce to admire or purchase.

Golf. **Carnation Golf Course,** 1810 W. Snoqualmie River Rd. NE; (425) 333-4151 or (877) 205-6106. Nestled in the bucolic Snoqualmie Valley, at the foothills of the Cascade Mountains. Noteworthy is the adjacent 100-acre wildlife preservation reserve, which means golfers can view osprey, peregrine falcons, and belted kingfishers as they play the 18-hole course.

Museums. **Camlann Medieval Village,** 10320 Kelly Rd. NE; (425) 788-8624; www.camlann.org. Operating for 3 decades, this non-profit living history museum project re-creates the 14th century rural life of Somerset, England.

FALL CITY
Golf. **Snoqualmie Falls Golf Course,** 35109 SE Fish Hatchery Rd.; (425) 392-1276. Eighteen holes and gorgeous Mount Si as a backdrop.

    Tall Chief Golf Course, 1313 W. Snoqualmie River Rd. SE; (425) 222-5911. Twelve-hole course.

Theater. **Snoqualmie Falls Forest Theatre,** P.O. Box 249, Bellevue, WA 98024; (425) 736-7252; www.foresttheater.org. Outdoor dinner theater, weekends June through Labor Day. For dinner reservations, call (425) 222-7044.

ISSAQUAH
Parks. **Lake Sammamish State Park,** www.parks.wa.gov/parks/? selectedpark=Lake%20Sammamish. From I-90, drive east to exit 5, and follow the signs to Lake Sammamish State Park, a 512-acre day-use park with 6,858 feet of waterfront and miles of hiking and biking trails. You can also rent kayaks. At the nearby creek, you can see the great blue heron rookery, or breeding grounds.

***Museums.* Gilman Town Hall Museum,** 165 SE Andrews St.; (425) 392-3500; www.issaquahhistory.org/townhall. Originally the town hall for old Issaquah, this little museum has some unusual artifacts, such as an authentic dynamite blaster and a rare Native American fur trade knife. Open Thurs through Sat, 11 a.m. to 3 p.m.

Issaquah Depot Museum, 50 Rainier Blvd., Issaquah; (425) 392-3500; www.issaquahhistory.org/depot/cars.htm. A fine museum that delights railroad aficionados and history buffs alike, who delight in numerous old train cars, a display of a stationmaster's desk, and an antique freight room. Open Fri through Sun, 11 a.m. to 3 p.m., and Thurs from 4 to 8 p.m. during the summer.

NORTH BEND

***Farms.* Meadowbrook Farm Preserve,** 1711 Boalch Ave.; (425) 831-1900; www.meadowbrookfarmpreserve.org. Off SR 202, with 460 acres of scenic and historic significance and a new interpretive center.

***Golf.* Mount Si Golf Course,** 9010 SE Boalch Rd.; (425) 391-4926. Voted one of the top 10 in the greater Seattle area.

***Museums.* Snoqualmie Valley Historical Museum,** 320 Bendigo Blvd. S; (425) 888-3200; www.snoqualmievalleymuseum.org. Open 1 to 5 p.m. Thurs through Sun, April through Oct (or by appointment). Fifty-year-old museum started by a former grade school teacher in the community takes a respectful look at pioneer lifestyles, the logging industry, and the contributions of the Snoqualmie tribe.

Other Recommended Restaurants and Lodging . . . .

CARNATION

Casa Vermillion Bed and Breakfast, 36517 NE 91st Way; (425) 333-5556; www.casavermillion.com. Three reasonably priced rooms in a spacious home surrounded by views of the Cascade foothills, Cascade Mountain Range, and Mount Rainier. Restful forest walks in the vicinity. Continental breakfast during the week and full breakfast on weekends.

ISSAQUAH

JaK's Grill, 14 Front St. N; (425) 837-8834; www.jaksgrill.com. Recipient of a variety of foodie awards, this eatery serves dinner every night, and lunch Tues through Sun. Best known for its high-quality beef, but the menu includes fish and chicken entrees and several varieties of salads as well.

Triple XXX Rootbeer Drive-in, 98 NE Gilman Blvd.; (425) 392-1266; www.triplexrootbeer.com. Loaded with souvenirs and paraphernalia from the '50s and '60s. Chicken and fish sandwiches and burgers named after favorite cars of that era.

The Old Hen Bed & Breakfast, 47150 SE 162nd St.; (425) 996-4119; www.theoldhen.org/home.html. Three suites, 2 with private baths, all lovingly furnished.

NORTH BEND

George's Bakery, 127 W. North Bend Way; (425) 888-0632. Popular with doughnut fans and other customers hankering for a home-made calzone or flatbread topped with cheese and tomatoes.

North Bend Bar & Grill, 145 E. North Bend Way; (888) 697-5016; www.northbendbarandgrill.com. Serves a wide range of breakfast, lunch, and dinner options, for meat eaters, vegetarians, and picky kids, too.

Roaring River Bed & Breakfast, 46715 SE 129th St.; (425) 888-4834 or (877) 627-4647; www.theroaringriver.com. Here are 3 rooms, a suite, and a cozy remodeled cabin called Herb's Place. Outstanding views of the middle fork of the Snoqualmie River. Proprietors deliver warm breakfast baskets to each unit.

Twede's Cafe, 137 E. North Bend Way; (425) 831-5511; www.twedes cafe.com. Breakfast and brunch diner that is best known as the TV program *Twin Peaks* eatery, where characters devoured cherry pie.

SNOQUALMIE
KoKo Beans Coffee House, 8010 Railroad Ave.; (425) 888-0259. A perfect spot for a good cup of coffee and one of its famous cinnamon scones or Aztec brownies. Open every day.

Salish Lodge and Spa, 6501 Railroad Ave. SE; (425) 888-2556 or (800) 272-5474; www.salishlodge.com. The lodge's dining room receives accolades for serving succulent smoked game and salmon, while the Attic Bistro's king salmon chowder and fire-roasted rib eye steaks tantalize the taste buds in a less formal setting. In fair weather the outdoor Kayak Cafe Bistro serves Dungeness crab salad and gourmet sandwiches. On the *Condé Nast Traveler* list again in 2010, Salish Lodge and Spa is considered one of the "world's best places to stay." The establishment has earned kudos as a haven for both celebratory events and personal retreats. Reservations are a must. Step into one of 89 guest rooms, each with its own whirlpool tub, wood-burning fireplace, feather bed, and custom-built furniture. No small detail goes unnoticed, from the luxury soaps to bedtime chocolates.

Snoqualmie Falls Candy Factory & Cafe, 8102 Railroad Ave.; (425) 888-0439 or (800) 636-2263; www.snofallscandy.com/factory .htm. For old-fashioned malts, and burgers, or a bag of candy.

Special Events . . . .

MAY THROUGH SEPTEMBER
Carnation Farmers' Market. A large market for a small community, selling garden plants, floral bouquets, fresh dairy products, berries, and other fruit. Lots of baked goods and other snacks.

JUNE
Annual Greenway Days, North Bend, http://mtsgreenway.org/about. A weekend celebration that brings people together to enjoy the scenic, recreational, and historic treasures in the area.

AUGUST
Snoqualmie Days, Snoqualmie. Arts and crafts booths, a parade, music, food concessions, children's games, and helicopter rides.

For More Information . . . .

Greater Issaquah Chamber of Commerce, 155 NW Gilman, Issaquah, WA 98027; (425) 392-7024; www.issaquahchamber.com.

Snoqualmie Valley Chamber of Commerce, P.O. Box 357, North Bend, WA 98045; (425) 888-4440; www.snovalley.org.

Washington State Parks, (360) 902-8844; www.parks.wa.gov. For more information on the many good hiking trails near Snoqualmie.

EASTBOUND ESCAPE *Three*

North Cascades

TRAVELING MIGHTY PEAKS AND IMMENSE GLACIERS / 2 NIGHTS

Alpine meadows

318 glaciers

Three-level antiques mall

Majestic viewpoints

North Cascades National Park

Old West towns

The North Cascades are often called the American Alps because of their jagged peaks, immense glaciers, and high meadows splashed with summer wildflowers. The wilderness around them, the 505,000-acre North Cascades National Park, is bisected by only one road, providing a remarkable retreat from crowded streets into natural beauty.

Along the route through the park, and on the occasional side roads that extend from it, you'll encounter numerous opportunities for outdoor adventure. This 3-day trip suggests a few. It's a summer or fall excursion, as much of the road is closed in winter. To reach the skiing areas mentioned during the ski season, you have to take a different route, approaching from the south.

DAY 1 / MORNING

Travel north from Seattle on SR 9 to Snohomish, about 30 miles. The river town, founded in 1859 on the banks of the Snohomish and Pilchuck Rivers, is one of Washington's oldest communities. It's thus fitting that Snohomish not only has examples of Victorian architecture but is also known as the antiques capital of the Northwest. Dozens of shops, many within a 4-block radius, sell antiques of all kinds.

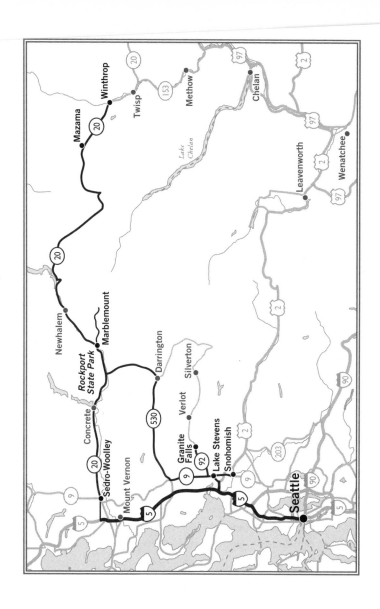

But before you begin browsing, give yourself a jump-start at **The Maltby Cafe,** 8809 Maltby Rd. (425-483-3123; www .maltbycafe.com), just outside of Snohomish. Voted "Best Breakfast in Western Washington," this plain-looking cafe is located in the basement of a former schoolhouse. Customers come from miles around; you can expect a long wait on the weekend. The scrambles, the country potatoes, and the fresh orange juice are favorites, and the tender homemade cinnamon rolls are enormous.

The 3-level **Star Center Antique Mall,** 829 2nd St. (360-568-2131), houses 150 dealers who sell everything from native artifacts to art nouveau. The mall is open every day. **Snohomish Antique Station,** 1108 1st St. (360-568-4913), represents 20 dealers offering glassware, furniture, china, and collectibles.

At the **Blackman House Museum,** 118 Ave. B (360-568-5235), you can see how many of these antiques were used in daily life. Open Sat and Sun, from noon to 3 p.m.

Now head north from Snohomish on SR 9 toward Lake Stevens. With 8 miles of shoreline and sandy beaches, you may want to dawdle at the lake for a spell. When autumn settles in, stop by the **Lake Stevens Historical Museum,** 1802 124th Ave. NE (425-334-3944), in the heart of downtown Lake Stevens. The historic timber equipment captures the interest of children and adults. Continue east, following the South Fork of the Stillaguamish River to Granite Falls on SR 92. If you are passing through on a Sunday, stop by the **Granite Falls History Museum,** 109 East Union St. (360-691-2603; www.gfhistory.org), open noon to 5 p.m. This small museum emphasizes Northwest industrial history, including railroads, logging, and mining. But you'll also find a doctor's office, a millinery shop, and a hardware store.

LUNCH   **Burger Barn,** 1020 Emens Ave N; (360) 436-2070. Of course, this is a fast-food burger joint, but the burgers, fries, and shakes are definitely a notch above average, and are guaranteed to fill you up for your afternoon drive.

AFTERNOON

This scenic route through Granite Falls, known as the Mountain Loop Highway (part of it is closed in winter), leads you through the logging town of Robe and the evergreen forests of Boulder River Wilderness. A few miles east is the **Verlot Ranger Station** (360-691-7791), which is just across the road from 5,324-foot **Mount Pilchuck.** The station provides maps and suggestions for hiking on the mountain. Snow often lingers through June, so it's best to ask at the ranger station about trail conditions if you are an enthusiastic, albeit occasional, hiker. The 7-mile road leading to the trail up the mountain is east of Verlot. From the trailhead, the hike up Mount Pilchuck is 2½ miles and leads to **Mount Pilchuck Lookout.** From here you gain one of the finest viewing points for scenic splendor in the state.

Just in front of you is the heart of Boulder River Wilderness, and the old mining town of Silverton, the only town you will pass within this dense forest. Just past Silverton is a sign that says **Big Four Mountain.** At the base of the immense escarpment, which soars 6,120 feet, a popular inn once stood. It was destroyed by fire long ago, but the site is a good picnic spot and leads visitors to a boardwalk that provides an easy passage through a bog and beaver pond. There's a short bridge across Ice Creek, from which you can follow the trail to the **Big Four Ice Caves.** The caves are said to be the lowest-lying glacier in the contiguous United States. The ¼-mile-long ice field is fed from a snow cone on Big Four. Do not enter these ice caves, which are susceptible to collapse.

Mountain Loop Highway will veer west again even as as it approaches the town of Darrington on SR 530. Continue now over Barlow Pass (elevation 2,600 feet), turning north to travel beside the tumultuous South Fork of the **Sauk River** for 19 miles to Darrington. The road is unpaved, but it's well graded.

The slate-blue Sauk is a favorite with whitewater rafters and kayakers because of its swift rapids. Through the trees on this narrow, winding road you'll glimpse mountain peaks—Sloan, Pugh, and White Chuck—and the Monte Cristo Range in Henry M. Jackson Wilderness. The Monte Cristo area was once the site of gold, copper, and silver mines.

When you reach Rockport, you'll see **Rockport State Park** on the bank of the Skagit River. The attractive park has campsites and a network of trails, partially accessible to wheelchairs. Gaze at old-growth Douglas firs and wander through the "ghost campground," closed by the state because one falling branch from the mammoth trees could crush a tent or RV.

On the western border of the park, a 7-mile road winds up **Sauk Mountain,** leading to **Sauk Mountain Trail.** On this trail take a 90-minute walk, one that is considered by many hikers to be one of the most beautiful in the North Cascades, with wildflowers and panoramic views from the mountain in the spring and summer. You may see hang gliders here.

After your hike, drive 8 miles northeast on SR 20 to your night's lodging in **Marblemount,** keeping an eye out for eagles, especially between Rockport State Park and Marblemount. In Marblemount you can pick up maps and backcountry permits and gasoline—this is the last gas stop for 75 miles.

DINNER   **Buffalo Run Restaurant,** 60084 SR 20, Marblemount; (360) 873-2461; www.buffaloruninn.com. An old-fashioned dining room that serves buffalo, venison, and elk, more conventional chicken and beef dishes, as well as homemade pie.

LODGING **Buffalo Inn,** 60117 SR 20; (360) 873-2103. A historic 1889 cedar roadhouse that once serviced miners and lumberjacks and now is a bed-and-breakfast with homespun rooms as well as a less expensive bunkhouse option. Complimentary breakfast.

DAY 2 / MORNING

BREAKFAST Enjoy expansive views and a full breakfast in the **Buffalo Run Restaurant and Inn** dining room.

Take the picnic lunch the innkeepers have packed for you (request this in advance), and drive east on SR 20, along the North Cascades Highway. Considered the most scenic mountain drive in Washington, this route is closed in winter.

SR 20 and the Skagit River flowing beside it divide the northern portion of North Cascades National Park from its southern part. There are almost no other roads in the national park, a wonderland of high mountains, jagged ridges, countless waterfalls, and glacially sculpted valleys. There are 318 glaciers in the park, more than half of all the glaciers in the contiguous United States. On off-road trails, you'll hear crashing icefalls and see broad snowfields and flower-dotted slopes.

Two short walks are located near the manicured village of Newhalem: the **Trail of the Cedars Bridge** is a nature walk that starts from a suspension bridge, is wheelchair accessible, and has interpretive signs that explain the forest's growth. The **Ladder Creek Rock Garden** is a ¼-mile trail that winds up a hillside, passing fountains and landscaped plantings to reach Ladder Creek Falls.

LUNCH **Picnic in Newhalem** or along the trail, or eat at **Buffalo Run Restaurant** in Marblemount.

AFTERNOON

To reach **Diablo Dam Trail,** turn off at milepost 126 for Diablo, cross Stetattle Creek, turn right at the fork in the road, and continue past the Diablo Powerhouse, community hall, and railway office to the signed trailhead (about 1½ miles from SR 20). The richly diverse **Diablo Lake Trail** is 7.6 miles round-trip and has an elevation gain of 1,500 feet. About 2 miles from the trailhead, a small trail turns right and leads to a dramatic view of Diablo Lake, as well as Sourdough Mountain, Davis Peak, Colonial Peak, Pyramid Peak, and the Skagit River.

This area is a pleasant lunch spot and a great place to look for bald eagles, red-tailed Cooper's, and sharp-shinned hawks. The longer hike offers a gentle climb through rich and varied habitats, including mature fir forests, mixed deciduous growth, and rocky outcroppings touching the open sky. For more information, contact the North Cascades National Park at Wilderness Information Center (360-873-4500).

Visit **Diablo Lake** viewpoints to ooh and aah over turquoise water colored by glacial flour, the fine-grained particles of rock. The paved, flat 1-mile path is accessible to all, winding through a forest pungent with alpine fir resin, and ending at a pretty lake with a ribbon waterfall.

Continue in a leisurely fashion on SR 20, stopping at the numerous turnouts to admire particularly striking views of ridges and green valleys.

Beyond Diablo is **Ross Lake,** its blue-green glacial waters extending far north into the wilderness, across the Canadian border. The only access to the lake is by boat or trail.

Ross Lake is named after James Ross, the engineer who designed dams on the Skagit River. Another Ross, Alexander, explored the southern section of the present park in 1814. After him came more explorers, then miners (mining efforts were abandoned because of the arduous terrain) and a few homesteaders. The dams were built in the 1930s and '40s by Seattle City Light to generate electricity.

Rainy Pass has an elevation of 4,860 feet. It's crossed by the Pacific Crest National Scenic Trail. Near the Rainy Lake rest stop is the **Rainy Lake National Recreation Trail,** a 1-mile paved path, wheelchair accessible, that leads to Rainy Lake. There's a memorable view here of the subalpine lake and waterfall streaming in from snowfields.

For a splendid close-up view of the Cascades, don't miss the **Washington Pass Overlook** (elevation 5,400 feet). **Liberty Bell Mountain** soars 7,808 feet above the valley. Next to it, almost as high, are the **Early Winter Spires;** Silver Star Mountain rises a steep 8,875 feet on the east. Against the dark ridges and snow-filled ravines, the leaves of Lyall's larch glow a brilliant yellow.

Now, as the road descends east of the Cascades into Washington's dry side, the scenery changes. There are no dense rain forests, thick with ferns and mosses; the vegetation thins, and firs give way to widely spaced pines. To the north lie the mountains and forests of the rugged, roadless Pasayten Wilderness. In recent years wolves have been found living deep in the wild—a welcome comeback, since they were thought to have disappeared.

Twelve miles from Washington Pass you'll come to **Mazama,** a popular ski center.

DINNER **Mazama Country Inn,** 15 Country Rd.; (509) 996-2681 or, within Washington, (800) 843-7951; www.mazamacountryinn.com. Pasta, chicken, and barbecued ribs are favorites here. The several varieties of burgers include elk and lamb. Light suppers of soup, salad, and bread available.

LODGING   **Mazama Country Inn.** Spacious cedar lodge, 18 simple but immaculate rooms. No phones, no TVs—no interruptions. Stone fireplace in living/dining area, windows on 3 sides offering views of forest. More than a dozen cabins and vacation homes with full kitchens are available. Bicycle rentals and horseback rides.

DAY 3 / MORNING

BREAKFAST   **Mazama Country Inn.** The lodge serves 3 meals a day (included in the American Plan rates in winter only).

Drive 13 miles east on SR 20 from Mazama, and you'll arrive in **Winthrop,** a town nestled in the upper Methow Valley, carved by glaciers 11,000 years ago. Farmers' fields, punctuated with rocky outcroppings, extend from the meandering Methow River. The river banks are outlined by poplar and ponderosa pines.

The town of Winthrop is almost surrounded by national forest-land. Here migrant Native American tribes once camped along the river, digging for camas root and fishing for salmon. White settlers and miners arrived after 1883.

When you visit Winthrop, you might think the townsfolk never left the late 1800s. The entire town has a frontier motif, with boardwalks, Old West storefronts, and saloon replicas.

Guy Waring and his wife and two children were among the early settlers. They came from Massachusetts and named the town after the governor of that state, John Winthrop. The Warings' home, built in 1897 after most of the town was destroyed by fire, is now the **Shafer Museum,** 285 Castle Ave. (509-996-2712; www.shafermuseum .com). It contains historical artifacts, wagons, and a stagecoach. Open Thurs through Mon, 10 a.m. to 5 p.m., Memorial Day weekend through Labor Day.

With 300 days of sunshine a year and an abundance of lakes, forests, mountainous terrain, and clean country air, the Methow Valley offers virtually limitless outdoor recreation. Fishing, photography, boating, river rafting, and skiing are among the most popular activities.

LUNCH **Old Schoolhouse Brewery,** 155 Riverside; (509) 996-3183; www.oldschoolhousebrewery.com. Salads, wraps, and burgers, including a meatless variety. Children's menu. Microbrews include an award-winning stout.

AFTERNOON

After lunch, stop by a gallery or two in Winthrop. The **Winthrop Gallery,** 237 Riverside Ave. (509-996-3925; www.winthropgallery .com), displays pastel paintings, photographs, enamelwork, and photography, and the **Ashford Gallery** on SR 20 (509-996-2073) has wearable art and practical art for dining tables. Replenish your reading material at **Trails End Bookstore,** 231 Riverside Ave. (509-996-2345; www.trailsendbookstore.com).

Stop by **Sheri's Sweet Shop,** 207 Riverside Ave. (509-996-3834), for dessert or to refuel on ice cream, some of which is made on the premises. Other options are the **Rocking Horse Bakery,** 265 Riverside Ave. (509-996-4241), for coffee and cookies. And 11 miles down the road in **Twisp** is **Cinnamon Twisp Bakery,** 116 N. Glover St. (509-997-5030; www.cinnamontwisp.com), an attractive bakery and cafe that also serves sandwiches on its organic whole-grain breads. Nearby is **Confluence Gallery and Art Center,** 104 Glover St. (www.confluencegallery.com), a nonprofit that hosts 7 exhibits by regional artists each year. The gift shop has a stylish collection of wearable art, pottery, books, and jewelry.

Once you are ready to return home, continue westward on SR 20 toward Sedro-Woolley. At Burlington, join I-5 for the 45-minute drive south to Seattle.

There's More . . . .

Boating. Ross Lake provides superb high-country wilderness canoeing. From Ross Dam parking lot, portage your canoe down a ¾-mile trail. You can choose to paddle to Ross Dam from Diablo Lake; for a fee, Ross Lake Resort in Rockport (206-386-4437) will haul you up to the lake.

Farms. Cascadian Farm, 55749 SR 20, Rockport; (800) 624-4123; www.cascadianfarm.com/Default.aspx. In the summer, stop by 28-acre Cascadian Farm and Roadside Stand in Rockport, where you can buy organic ice cream, a bag of fruit, or organic snacks such as granola bars, honey nut snack mix, or spiced cereal trail mix.

Fishing. At Baker Lake, fish for kokanee, and at Lake Stevens fish for bullhead and yellow perch. At Ross, Diablo, and Gorge Lakes, try for native, naturally occurring rainbow trout.

Horseback riding. Horse Country Farm, 8507 SR 92, Granite Falls; (360) 691-7509. Trail rides in the Cascade foothills, along the Pilchuck River. Ponies, riding lessons, family trail rides, and spring and summer camps are also available.

Skiing. Methow Valley Sport Trails Association, 209 Castle Ave., Winthrop; (509) 996-3287. Provides information and maps on Nordic ski trails in Sun Mountain, Rendezvous, and Mazama areas. MVSTA also gives recorded updates on trail conditions on more than 200 kilometers of all-season trails throughout the Methow Valley.

Wineries. Glacier Peak Winery and Tasting Room, 58575 SR 20, Rockport; (360) 873-4073; www.glacierpeakwinery.com. Located east of Rockport at milepost 104. Visit the new tasting room and of course the winery, nestled between mountain peaks and a glacier.

Special Events . . . .

JULY

Bluegrass Festival, Darrington. The Darrington Bluegrass Music Park sits right at the base of Whitehorse Mountain, which is surrounded by Mount Baker National Forest. In this setting, bluegrass aficionados meet and jam, sometimes around the clock, in addition to performing for crowds of fans from around the Northwest. For more information, check out www.glacierview.net/bluegrass.

Winthrop Rhythm & Blues Festival, www.winthropbluesfestival .com. The performances at this 3-day event are almost nonstop at the Blues Ranch, just west of Winthrop.

LATE SEPTEMBER

Historical Society Home Tour, Snohomish. This event is sponsored by the Snohomish Historical Society and is a tour of Victorian city homes, stylish farm homes, parsonages, and the local train depot.

EARLY OCTOBER

Granite Falls Railroad Days, Granite Falls. Celebrates the era of steam trains in the region. There's a traditional Main Street parade, and also a spaghetti dinner and Saturday evening dance, plus egg tosses, duck and bed races, and other outrageously silly competitive sports.

OCTOBER

Festival of Pumpkins, Snohomish. Hay rides, corn mazes, petting zoos, and (watch out) a pumpkin hurl.

Great Pumpkin River Race and Celebration, downtown Snohomish. This couldn't be considered your standard race, with racing pumpkins vying for the prize.

Other Recommended Restaurants and Lodging . . . .

CONCRETE
Ovenells' Heritage Inn, 46276 Concrete Sauk Valley Rd.; (360) 853- 8494; www.ovenells-inn.com. The main inn has 4 antiques-filled rooms, while the pine log cabins are brand-new, with vaulted ceilings. The Bear Hollow Guest House is also new and comes with a fully equipped kitchen.

DARRINGTON
Darrington Motor Inn, 1100 Seeman St.; (360) 436-1776. Pleasantly furnished, large rooms, some with kitchenettes. Laundry facilities, and views of Whitehorse Mountain.

MARBLEMOUNT
The Eatery Drive-in at Clark's Skagit River Cabins (aka Skagit River Resort), SR 20 near Marblemount, Milepost 103.5, North Cascades Highway; (360) 873-2250 or (800) 273-2606; www.northcascades.com. Stop by for giant cinnamon rolls baked by 90-something Tootsie Clark from a brown sugar–raisin-walnut and butter-packed recipe passed down from her mother.

ROCKPORT
Ross Lake Resort, 503 Diablo St., Rockport; (206) 386-4437; www.rosslakeresort.com. Large and small cabins and a 2-story bunkhouse. Towels, bedding, and pots and pans supplied but bring your own food, because there are no restaurants or stores nearby.

SNOHOMISH

Snohomish Inn, 323 2nd St.; (360) 568-2208 or (800) 548-9993; www.snohomishinn.com. Offers basic amenities in sparkling-clean rooms.

TWISP

Methow Valley Inn, 234 2nd St.; (509) 997-2253; www.methow valleyinn.com. Beautiful old home painted white with green trim. Eight rooms, 5 en suite and 3 with a shared bath. All clean and cozy, with comfortable side chairs and hand-crafted quilts. Full breakfast.

Tappi, 201 Glover St.; (509) 997-3345. A first-rate Italian restaurant that is very popular for its pizza but renowned among foodies for its chicken and meat entrees. Dinner only.

WINTHROP

Arrowleaf Bistro, 253 Riverside Ave.; (509) 996-3919; www.arrow leafbistro.com/index.php. A friendly neighborhood restaurant that sticks to regional and local ingredients. Serves small plates, beef and chicken entrees for dinner, and an inspired Sunday brunch.

Duck Brand Hotel and Cantina, 248 Riverside Ave.; (509) 996-2192; www.methownet.com/duck. Mexican dishes, as well as sandwiches, steaks, pies, and chocolate cake. Also serves breakfast. The hotel has 6 reasonably priced rooms.

Hotel Rio Vista, 285 Riverside Ave.; (509) 996-3535; www.hotel riovista.com. Pleasant Eastern-style decor in large rooms, with decks overlooking the Methow and Chewuch Rivers.

Sun Mountain Lodge, 604 Patterson Lake Rd.; (509) 996-2211 within Washington, (800) 572-0493 outside Washington; www.sun

mountainlodge.com. Rustic establishment in the Methow Valley, has 96 rooms with mountain views in the log-beamed lodge and 16 cabins. Swimming pool, tennis courts, cross-country ski trails, and ice-skating rink. Dining room serves breakfast, lunch, and dinner. Wolf Creek Bar and Grill offers lighter fare.

For More Information . . . .

Concrete Chamber of Commerce, 45770 Main St., P.O. Box 743, Concrete, WA 98237; (360) 853-7621; www.concrete-wa.com /chamberofcommerce. Located in the Skagit County Community Resource Center.

North Cascades Chamber of Commerce, 59831 SR 20, P.O. Box 175, Marblemount, WA 98267-0175; (360) 873-2106 or (800) 875-2448; www.marblemount.com.

North Cascades National Park Visitor Center, (206) 386-4495, ext. 11; www.nps.gov/noca/planyourvisit/visitorcenters.htm.

Sedro-Woolley Chamber of Commerce, 714-B Metcalf St., Sedro-Woolley, WA 98284; (360) 855-1841; www.sedro-woolley.com.

Snohomish County Tourism Bureau, 909 SE Everett Mall Way, C300, Everett, WA 98208; (425) 348-5802 or (888) 338-0976; www.snohomish.org.

Twisp Chamber of Commerce, P.O. Box 686, Twisp, WA 98856; (509) 997-2020.

Winthrop Chamber of Commerce, 202 SR 20, Winthrop, WA 98862; (509) 996-2125 or (888) 463-8469; www.winthropwashington.com.

EASTBOUND ESCAPE *Four*

Leavenworth to Yakima

DISCOVERING THE STATE'S AGRICULTURAL BOUNTY /
2 NIGHTS

One of Seattle's great attractions is its proximity to magnificent mountainous wilderness. You can breakfast in a cosmopolitan restaurant and be deep in a silent forest by lunchtime. This 3-day getaway will take you east through the rugged North Cascades, into semiarid ranch country and among soft val-

> Bavarian village
> Fruit Bowl of the Nation
> Nutcracker museum
> Ranch country
> Water sports
> Wineries

leys where 60 percent of the nation's apples are grown. On the way you'll encounter breathtaking mountain scenery, rivers inviting whitewater adventure, trails that meander into dense forests, and a few surprises in between.

DAY 1 / MORNING

Drive north from Seattle on I-5 to SR 520 and I-405, headed toward Woodinville. Stop for a tour of the famed **Chateau Ste. Michelle Winery,** 14111 NE 145th St. (425-488-1133 or 800-267-6793; www
.ste-michelle.com), the state's leading winery in a turreted chateau.

Tours and tastings are available every day from 10 a.m. to 6 p.m. Stroll 87 acres of grounds landscaped with trout ponds, manicured lawns, formal gardens, experimental vineyards, and picnic tables.

North of the winery, join SR 522 headed northeast toward US 2. Traveling east on the scenic highway, you'll follow the **Skykomish River,** a ribbon of clear blue water that flows west from the high

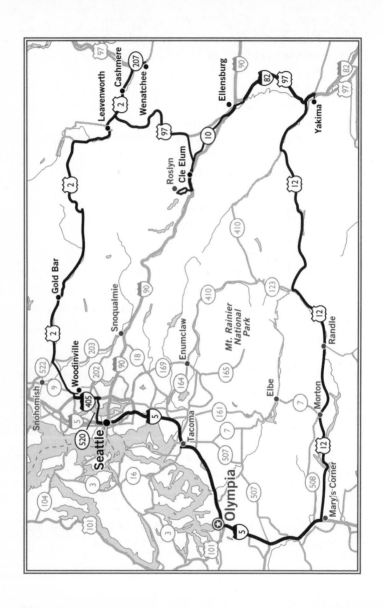

lakes of alpine wilderness. Popular with rafters for both its rapids and its serene stretches, the Skykomish offers steelhead fishing, riverside trails, gold panning, and float trips. Majestic eagles soar above, indifferent to all the activity.

Amid the new-growth forests found on either side of the river are the stumps of virgin old growth, long since logged. The stumps, some 6 feet in diameter, indicate the advanced age of these giants.

LUNCH   **Zeke's Drive In,** 44006 US 2, Gold Bar. This charming train car eatery serves huge, juicy burgers and onion rings that some people go out of their way to nosh on, but they also have fish and veggie options and make shakes in a dozen flavors.

AFTERNOON

Two miles east of Gold Bar, at **Wallace Falls State Park,** stop to hike the trail, which climbs to 1,200 feet and affords grand views of Wallace Falls, a 365-foot cascade. South of the Skykomish you'll see imposing **Mount Index,** nearly 6,000 feet high.

The next stop on the highway is the village of **Index** (population 157). It is a quaint assortment of dark-red clapboard buildings that include a historic tavern, museum, general store, city hall, and pioneer park, all clustered around the first corner as you cross the bridge into town.

Near Skykomish, a timber town that fills with hikers and backpackers in summer and with skiers in winter, you can take a short walk to **Deception Falls,** a tumbling waterfall that splashes down the mountainside and under the highway bridge. The Iron Goat Trail, Milepost 55 on US 2, follows the route where the Great Northern Railway cut through Stevens Pass in 1893. Walk past old, collapsed snow sheds, tunnels, and work campsites.

Continuing on US 2, you'll leave the Skykomish River and drive through coniferous forest, passing Alpine Falls and rising into the Cascade Mountains to Stevens Pass, at an elevation of 4,061 feet. One thousand feet below runs a 7-mile tunnel, the longest railroad tunnel in North America. If you walk from the summit to Stevens Pass Ski Area, you'll have a peerless view of the snowy peaks of the Cascade Range.

Descending now on the east side of the Cascades, drive 20 more miles to Coles Corner. From here, SR 207 leads 4 miles to **Lake Wenatchee State Park** (888-226-7688). This busy recreation area on the edge of Lake Wenatchee offers skiing, fishing, boating, and beaches.

Take US 2 through the **Tumwater Canyon,** along the bouncing, cascading Wenatchee River as it rushes toward the Columbia. In any season the landscape is lovely, but in autumn, when the woodlands blaze with color, it's particularly glorious.

Sixteen miles south of Coles Corner, in Icicle Valley, you'll enter **Leavenworth.** After the railroad moved and the town lost its economic base from timber in the '60s, the town reinvented itself to resemble a quaint Bavarian village, with chalets, carved railings, peaked gables, and a profusion of hanging flower baskets in the summer.

The combination of a European-style village and a spectacular alpine setting has contributed to a consistently healthy tourist-based economy, drawing visitors by the thousands every year to shop, gawk, eat, raft, rock climb, fish, and ski. If you are interested in picking up outdoor recreation maps, drop by the **Wenatchee River Ranger District,** 600 Sherbourne (509-548-2550 or 509-548-2551), in Leavenworth.

For the rest of the afternoon you might choose to hike, bird watch, or play golf. Or you might want to browse through the dozens of quaint shops. Begin with the **Cheesemonger's Shop,** 819

Front St. (509-548-9011 or 877-888-7389; www.cheesemongers shop.com), which sells cheeses, sausages, beers, and wines from around the worldand see artisans at work in the **Wood Carver Gallery,** 715-B Front St. (509-548-2064).

There are many attractive shops, but be sure to stop by **Wooly Bully Yarns** (509-548-0895 or 866-44WOOLY; www.woolybully yarns.com), a fiber arts shop selling fine yarns and knitting accessories. See as well the quilts at nearby **Dee's Country Accents,** 917 Commercial St. (800-253-8990); the 3,500 distinctive music boxes in **Die Musik Box,** 933 Front St. (509-548-6152; www.music boxshop.com); and the Christmas crafts at **Kris Kringl,** 907 Front St. (509-548-6867 or 888-557-4645; www.kkringl.com). Check out the **Leavenworth Nutcracker Museum,** which displays close to 6,000 nutcrackers of all vintages and designs, located at 735 Front St. (509-548-4708 or 800-892-3989) on the second floor above the **Nussknacker Haus** (www.nussknackerhaus.com), a retail outlet that sells nutcrackers. The museum, which has received attention on *Good Morning America* and other national media as a purveyor of nutcracker figurines, is open from 2 to 5 p.m. May through Oct, and on weekends only Nov through Apr.

Don't miss a walk along the Wenatchee River in tranquil **Waterfront Park,** off Commercial Street. Just a block and a half from the busy shopping area, the park is a quiet spot with benches, trees, and views of the river and the steep peaks around Icicle Canyon. The Wenatchee River is one of the state's most popular rafting rivers.

DINNER   **Visconti's,** 639 Front St.; (541) 548-1213; www.viscontis .com. Quality Italian dining. Recipient of *Wine Spectator* magazine's "Award of Excellence Restaurant" for the past 10 years. Serving lunch and dinner every day. A host of creative Italian entrees and pasta dishes, prime rib, and antipasti plates.

LODGING **Autumn Pond Bed and Breakfast,** 10388 Titus Rd.; (509) 548-4482 or (800) 222-9661. Rests on 3 quiet country acres, surrounded by panoramic views of the majestic Cascades. Guests can relax on a wooden swing by the private pond or in an outdoor hot tub. Six guest rooms, each with a private bath, queen bed, and country ranch decor. Common room has comfortable seating, games, and plenty of interesting reading material.

DAY 2 / MORNING

BREAKFAST A bountiful country breakfast is served in the open dining room at **Autumn Pond Bed and Breakfast.**

Continue on US 2 to **Peshastin,** a community prominent for its farm stands that are operated by local families. Several sell jams and jellies and candies that make nice gifts. Stop by, browse, and ask if you can visit the farm. Among them are **CRM Orchards/Miller Orchards** (www.millerorchards.com), **Nicholson Orchard** (www.our orchard.com/Home.aspx), **Prey's Fruit Barn** (www.preysfruitbarn .com), and **Smallwood's Harvest** (www.smallwoodsharvest.com). Drive ahead on US 2 to **Cashmere,** passing miles of apple orchards that are clouds of white and pink in spring and are laden with fruit in fall. Apples are big business in Washington; 7 billion are grown annually, 60 percent of the nation's apple production.

In Cashmere, at Liberty Acres, just off US 2, is the **Aplets and Cotlets manufacturing plant,** 117 Mission St. (509-663-0711 or 800-888-5696). Take the brief tour and watch the making of the famous fruit-and-nut confections.

Not to be missed is the **Historic Museum and Pioneer Village,** 600 Cotlets Way (509-782-3230; www.cashmeremuseum.org /museum.html), where you step from the highway into the past. Highlights inside the museum are the basketry and beadwork of the local Wenatchee First Nations tribes. On the museum grounds, a typical pioneer village, complete with blacksmith shop, mission, assay office, saloon, dentist's office, hotel, millinery shop, and jailhouse, is open to the public.

From Cashmere, drive to **Cle Elum,** taking US 97 south then SR 970 west. Once a coal-mining and railroad town, it's now a gateway to mountain and lake outdoor recreation. Stop at the **Cle Elum Bakery,** 501 E. 1st St. (509-674-2233), for caramel-nut rolls and coffee. Also check out **Glondo's Sausage Company,** 216 E. 1st St. (509-674-5755; www.glondossausage.com), for Yugoslav sausage and Polish kielbasa. Almost every town has its special museum; Cle Elum preserves phone history in the **Cle Elum Historical Telephone Museum,** 221 E. 1st St. (509-674-5702). Another interesting spot is the **Carpenter Museum,** 302 W. 3rd St. (509-674-5702), a stately mansion that houses exhibits from life in the region's earlier days. Both museums have limited hours, so call first.

Now you are entering **Wenatchee,** the apple capital of the United States, and one of the world's largest producers of apples. The Wenatchee and Columbia Rivers meet here, giving the town numerous gathering spots along the rivers' edges. The 11-mile Apple Capital Loop Trail is one of the easiest ways to access the town's scenic river banks. **Wenatchee Valley Museum and Cultural Center,** 127 S. Mission St. (509-888-6240), in downtown Wenatchee, features out-of-the-ordinary displays. A coin-operated 1892 railroad diorama, aviation exhibits showing the historic 1931 transpacific crossing, a 9-rank Wurlitzer theater organ, and Native American artifacts are part of the disparate collection.

A side trip north on US 97 Alt., on the west bank of the river, leads you to the **Washington Apple Commission Visitor Center,** 2900 Euclid Ave. (509-663-9600). It's open daily May through December 23 and on weekdays the rest of the year. The gift shop is open Monday through Friday year-round. You'll get an in-depth look at the apple industry at the center, which sells souvenirs and pies, shows an 18-minute video, and offers free samples of Washington's famous apples. Continue north on US 97 Alt. to the nationally known **Ohme Gardens,** 3327 Ohme Rd. (509-662-5785), where you can look down on the junction of the Wenatchee and Columbia Rivers. Drive on another few miles to **Rocky Reach Dam Park** at its visitor center on the west side of the dam, accessible from exit 97A (509-663-7522; www.chelanpud.org and http://rockyreachdam .com). On the premises are a historic gallery displaying 10,000 years of natural history, a fish viewing room, and award-winning landscaping. Open daily March 1 through mid-November, 9 a.m. to 4 p.m., depending on weather conditions.

Before leaving Wenatchee, stop for lunch.

LUNCH **McGlinn's Public House Restaurant,** located in the historic Garland Building, 111 Orondo Ave.; (509) 663-9073; www.mcglinns.com. Delicious wood-fired pizzas, some with unusual combinations of ingredients that work: peaches and prosciutto, for example, or Thai curry chicken and bean sprouts. Their specialty sandwiches include roast beef with blue cheese, Greek gyros with lamb, and grilled chicken with cranberry chutney.

AFTERNOON

Drive south on US 97, leaving the orchards for the forests of the Wenatchee Mountains. Then descend into arid cowboy country. The climate here is hot and dry in the summer, while winters are harsh, with far more snowfall than occurs west of the Cascade Range.

The scenic route, over the old Blewett Pass Road, is narrow and winding and closed in winter. It is a shortcut that leaves, then rejoins, US 97, which is open all year.

When you reach **Ellensburg,** stop at the chamber of commerce on Sprague Street for a walking-tour map of the historic downtown. It's full of interesting architecture, with redbrick buildings dating from the late 1800s, an art deco theater, and modern structures on the Central Washington University campus. Antiques shops abound, along with stores selling the famous **Ellensburg Blue agate,** found only in this region.

Don't miss a visit to the museum of Ellensburg native John Clymer, nationally known cover artist for the *Saturday Evening Post* magazine, so popular in the early 20th century. The **Clymer Museum** is located inside the **Kittitas County Historic Museum,** 114 E. 3rd St. (509-925-3778; www.kchm.org), which maintains more than 8,500 objects in its collections, among them Native American basketry, stone tools, and household items from Ellensburg's earliest settlements. But Clymer's original paintings and sketches remain the highlight of this visit. From an early age Clymer was mesmerized by the Wild West, and much of his work reflects the people and wildlife of those landscapes. Yet he was a versatile professional who managed to make a living as a cover artist; he depicted American family life with great, perhaps idyllic, reverence. Many of his magazine covers are on display.

DINNER   **Valley Cafe,** 105 W. 3rd, Ellensburg; (509) 925-3050. Art deco surroundings, and chicken and seafood entrees served with flair: potato-crusted ahi tuna, spicy Thai peanut chicken, and crab cakes topped with caper-tomato relish. They make their own breads and have an extensive Northwest wine list.

LODGING   **The Wren's Nest Bed & Breakfast,** 300 E. Manitoba Ave.; (509) 925-9061; www.wrensnest.com. Antiques-furnished guest rooms. Easy walk to Central Washington University and historic downtown Ellensburg.

DAY 3 / MORNING

....

BREAKFAST   The Wren's Nest Bed & Breakfast provides a full gour-met breakfast with egg and meat dishes, waffles, Swedish pancakes, and fresh-baked bread.

Drive south on US 97 to **Yakima.** For more than a century, this region has relied on an agricultural economy for its livelihood, hence its unchallenged title of **"The Fruit Bowl of the Nation."** Yet these days, many people think of Yakima Valley primarily as the heart of wine country. Both are true. Cherry, apple, and pear orchards still cover the valley floor, but now vineyards also carpet the region in rhythmic patterns. For the **Yakima Wine Association**'s listing of more than 50 wineries that call Yakima home, see www.wineyakimavalley.org.

Once you are in Yakima city, drop by the **Yakima Valley Museum,** 2105 Tieton Dr. (509-248-0747; www.yakimavalleymuseum.org). This surprisingly large museum has excellent permanent and rotat-ing exhibits. The permanent exhibits on the region's Native Ameri-can culture, the valley's fruit industry, and the interactive Children's Underground are well worth an hour or more. If you plan to picnic, visit the **Yakima Greenway,** along the Yakima River. You will find 10 miles of trails, 3,600 acres of natural habitat, and 2 pleasant parks. The heart of downtown Yakima, between First and Second Avenues, offers a good selection of shops and restaurants: North Town Coffeehouse, Mel's Diner, Second Street Grill, Bob's Keg and Cork, and Tony's Steak House.

LUNCH   Tony's Steak House, 221 W. Yakima Ave.; (509) 853-1010; www.tonysteakhouse.com. Delicious starters and salads if you just want something light before driving home. Burgers, wraps, and sandwiches make up the heartier fare.

Leave Yakima by following SR 12 west to I-5.

There's More . . . .

ELLENSBURG

Tours. **Olmstead Place State Park,** 921 N. Ferguson Rd.; (509) 925-1943. Southeast of Ellensburg off I-90. you can step into one of the first farms in Kittitas Valley. There's a log cabin, built in 1875, and several buildings, including a barn and schoolhouse. Open for tours in the summer on weekends, 12 to 5 p.m., Memorial Day through Labor Day,

    Thorp Grist Mill, 11640 N. Thorp Hwy; (509) 964-9640; www .thorp.org. Built back in 1883 when Ellensburg (then called Robbers' Roost) was booming, the 4-story mill provided flour and jobs to many residents in the region, and was fully operational until 1946. Lovingly maintained by the community, the mill is nicely preserved and one of the few remaining in the state. To get there, take I-90 north to exit 101.

Wildlife. **Chimposium at the Chimpanzee and Human Communication Institute,** Central Washington University; (509) 963-2244. Reserve a Sat or Sun Mar through Nov. Watch chimps "talk" in sign language.

LEAVENWORTH

Bicycling. Bicycle routes for all abilities surround the Leavenworth area. Rent bicycles at **Der Sportsmann,** 837 Front St. (509-548-5623; www.dersportsmann.com) or **Das Rad Haus**, 1207 Front St. (509-548-5615; www.dasradhaus.com).

Golf. **Leavenworth Golf Club,** 9101 Icicle Rd.; (509) 548-7267. Established in 1927, and one of the oldest golf courses in the Pacific Northwest; 18 holes, with the North Cascades as a stunning backdrop.

Rafting. Raft the whitewater of the Wenatchee River with **Leavenworth Outfitters Inc.,** 325 Division; (509) 548-0368; www.leavenworth outfitters.com. Scenic float trips also available.

Osprey Rafting Company, 9342 Icicle Rd.; (800) 743-6269; www.ospreyrafting.com. Another outfitting option.

Shopping. **The Alps Candy,** 13901 US 2; (509) 548-4419. Fudge, gourmet foods, and gifts, such as homemade jams, syrups, and mustards.

Skiing. Cross-country ski trails are numerous in the Leavenworth/ Wenatchee area. **Icicle River Trail** and **Lake Wenatchee** are popular, and so are the golf course and city park in Leavenworth. For information call **Wenatchee National Forest,** (509) 548-6977.

Stevens Pass, (206) 812-4510. Open Nov to mid-Apr. Downhill skiers have access to 6 double chair lifts and 2 triples. Longest run is 6,047 feet.

WENATCHEE
Golf. **Rock Island Golf Course,** 314 Saunders Rd., Rock Island, east of Wenatchee; (509) 884-2806. Located along the Columbia River, this course has 9 holes, making it a good course for beginners or those who want a faster golf game.

Skiing. **Mission Ridge,** 7500 Mission Ridge Rd., (509) 663-6543; www.missionridge.com. Has 4 chair lifts and runs up to 5 miles long.

Special Events . . . .

LATE APRIL/EARLY MAY
Washington State Apple Blossom Festival, Wenatchee. Parades, carnival, arts-and-crafts fair.

MID-MAY
Maifest, Leavenworth. Maypole dance, bandstand entertainment, handbell ringers, outdoor breakfast, flea market, antiques bazaar, street dancing, and flower vendors.

EARLY JUNE
Founders Day, Cashmere. Celebrate the historic figures who first settled in the Northwest's apple country.

JUNE
Leavenworth International Accordion Celebration, Leavenworth. Old World architecture, flowering gardens, and artisans provide the backdrop for this musical celebration.

JULY
Yakima Folklife Festival, Yakima. Craft and food vendors. A mini medieval festival with music and dance on 5 outdoor stages.

EARLY SEPTEMBER
Chelan County Fair, Cashmere. Labor Day weekend. Offers all the best of a well-organized county fair, including animal shows, square-dancing demonstrations, and textile arts and floral displays.

SEPTEMBER
Ellensburg Rodeo. One of the major US rodeos. Four-day event, with cowhands competing for cash prizes. Also carnival rides, produce and craft displays, homemade pies, and music.

Leavenworth Crush Festival. Sample wines from 30 Washington wineries, eat terrific food, and listen to quality jazz. Get your feet wet—in grape juice. For a small fee, taste 15 of the 30 wines on hand and bring a glass home as a souvenir.

Wenatchee's Taste of Harvest Festival is a chance for the entire family to wander around the farmers' market, watch or participate in 10K and half marathon races, sample 8 wines for a small fee, gorge at a pancake breakfast, and listen to live music.

LATE SEPTEMBER

Autumn Leaf Festival, Leavenworth. Grand parade, accordion and oompah music, art displays, street dance, food booths, and a pancake breakfast.

Central WA State Fair. Weeklong agricultural fair with livestock exhibitions, concerts, a rodeo, food vendors, and carnival rides.

OCTOBER

Cashmere Apple Days, Cashmere. Pie-baking contest, races, music, dancing, and pioneer entertainment. A fund-raiser for Chelan County Museum.

LATE NOVEMBER

Thanksgiving in Wine Country. Numerous Yakima Valley wineries showcase their wines in food and wine pairings.

Christkindlmarkt, Leavenworth. A German-style Christmas village. Booths filled with holiday foods and gift items. Christmas music and an Olde World Puppet Theatre for children.

EARLY DECEMBER

Christmas Lighting, Leavenworth. Snowman contest, sledding, food booths, concerts, and the lighting of the village.

Other Recommended Restaurants and Lodging . . . .

CLE ELUM

The Cottage Cafe & Lounge, 911 E. 1st St.; (509) 674-2922; www .cottagecafecleelum.com. Open daily from 6 a.m. to midnight. Lunch menu offers several salads and sandwiches, and soups that change daily. There's an on-site bakery, for those who just want a snack of fresh pie, crisp, or cobbler.

Iron Horse Inn B&B, 526 Marie Ave., South Cle Elum; (509) 674-5939 or (800) 22-TWAIN. A former bunkhouse for railroad workers, restored as an attractive bed-and-breakfast with a railroad theme. Four genuine caboose cars have been lovingly renovated. All cars feature private baths, TV/DVD/VCR, microwaves, refrigerators, and outside sun decks. Full breakfast.

Suncadia Resort, 3600 Suncadia Trail; (509) 649-6400 or (866) 904-6301; www.suncadiaresort.com. The lodge offers full-service 1- and 2-bedroom guest suites, while 18 guest rooms and suites are available at the inn; rental homes are custom designed and fully furnished. Full-service spa on premises.

ELLENSBURG

The Inn at Goose Creek, 1720 Canyon Rd.; (509) 962-8030 or (800) 533-0822; www.innatgoosecreek.com. Ten rooms, some with Jacuzzi tubs. All with goose-down comforters and refrigerators. Filling continental breakfast bar, plus late-night snacks for the room.

Morelli's Cafe Italiano, 423 N. Main St.; (509) 925-7704. Tasty, homemade Italian bistro fare comes in large servings. Accommodates children's appetites.

Yellow Church Cafe, 111 S. Pearl; (509) 933-2233. This former little church, which was built for German Lutherans in 1923, serves breakfast, lunch, and dinner. Traditional breakfasts include eggs and pancakes; also available for breakfast are wraps and a berry granola cobbler. Lunch menu offers salads, soups, quiches, and sandwiches. Dinner fare includes steaks, chicken, pastas, and vegetarian dishes.

LEAVENWORTH

All Seasons River Inn, 8751 Icicle Rd.; (509) 548-1425 or (800) 254-0555; www.allseasonsriverinn.com. Adults only. Bed-and-breakfast with 6 spacious rooms. All but 1 room have whirlpool tubs. Private decks, river views, antiques, and a hearty breakfast.

Anna Hotel Pension, 926 Commercial; (509) 548-6273 or (800) 509-2662; www.pensionanna.com. Sixteen units in a Bavarian-style inn. Traditional European breakfast included.

Enzian Inn, 590 US 2; (509) 548-5269 or (800) 223-8511; www .enzianinn.com. Hotel with 104 rooms, combining Old World atmosphere with contemporary comfort. Heated pool, hot tub, some fireplaces. Full European buffet breakfast included.

Homefires Bakery, 11007 US 2; (509) 548-7362; www.homefires bakery.com. Freshly made whole-grain breads, European and specialty breads, pies, cinnamon rolls, and cookies, baked in a wood-fired masonry oven.

Mountain Home Lodge, 8201 Mountain Home Rd.; (509) 548-7077 or (800) 414-2378; www.mthome.com. Intimate getaway in roomy stone-and-wood lodge with pool. In the hills, 3 miles from town. Full breakfast included. During winter months, establishment serves all meals.

Pavz Creperie, 833 Front St.; (509) 548-2103. Crepes for breakfast, lunch, and dinner: strawberry crepes, portobello mushroom crepes, chicken and spinach crepes, crepes drizzled with chocolate and topped with ice cream, plus good coffee and good brews.

Run of the River, 9308 E. Leavenworth Rd.; (509) 548-7171 or (800) 288-6491. Bed-and-breakfast in a log lodge on the river, 1 mile from downtown. Six comfortable rooms, warm hospitality, deck with hot tub.

Sleeping Lady A Mountain Resort, 2½ miles from town at 7375 Icicle Rd.; (800) 574-2123. A 67-acre conference retreat center with guest rooms, gourmet meals, and music concerts in a natural setting. Listed in the 2009 *Condé Nast Traveler* Top 100 list. Ideal for larger groups. Two-night stay minimum for individuals.

PESHASTIN
Beecher Hill House, 9991 Beecher Hill Rd.; (509) 548-0559 or (866) 414-0559; www.beecherhill.com. The home of pioneer Samuel Beecher, built in 1910, is still very much a manor with a terraced garden and graceful home. Two suites and 2 rooms, a game room, and library.

ROSLYN
Brick Tavern, 100 E. Pennsylvania Ave.; (509) 649-2643; www.bricksaloon.com. Just a few miles away from Cle Elum, Brick Tavern is the second-oldest continuously operating saloon in Washington state, where the *Northern Exposure* television program was filmed. People make a special point of stopping for the tasty spaghetti, prime rib, and taco dinners. Roslyn is famous for its dozens of ethnic cemeteries, where miners are buried among their own cultural groups, banded together on a hillside west of town.

THORP

Rose Hill Farm Bed & Breakfast, 16161 N. Thorp Hwy.; (509) 964-2427 or (866) 279-0546. Located on a working farm situated along the Yakima River, the main house has 4 bedrooms, 2 of which have soaking tubs. Also on the premises are a small studio and tiny cottage. Hosts deliver a basket of fresh muffins to rooms; a full breakfast with hot entree follows.

WENATCHEE

The Ivywild Inn, 410 N. Miller; (509) 293-5517 or (866) 608-8808; www.theivywildinn.com. A 6,000-square-foot restored mansion with wireless Internet and flat-screen TV in each of the 4 rooms. Two-course breakfast. Range of cooking classes throughout the year.

Warms Springs Inn Bed and Breakfast, 1611 Love Lane; (509) 662-8365 or (800) 543-3645; www.warmspringsinn.com. Situated on 10 acres along the Wenatchee River. Six guest rooms in a 1917 mansion with spectacular grounds. Voted "Best Breakfast in the Northwest."

For More Information . . . .

Cashmere Chamber of Commerce, 204 Cottage St., P.O. Box 834, Cashmere, WA 98815; (509) 782-7404; www.cashmerechamber .com.

Cle Elum-Roslyn Chamber of Commerce, 401 W. 1st St., Cle Elum, WA 98922; (509) 674-5958; www.cleelumroslyn.org.

Ellensburg Chamber of Commerce, 609 N. Main St., Ellensburg, WA 98926; (509) 925-3138 or (888) 925-2204; www.ellensburg-chamber.com.

Greater Yakima Chamber of Commerce, 10 N. 9th St., Yakima, WA 98901-2590; (509) 248-2021; www.yakima.org.

Leavenworth Chamber of Commerce, P.O. Box 327, Leavenworth, WA 98826; (509) 548-5807; www.leavenworth.org.

Monroe Chamber of Commerce, 118 North Lewis St., Suite 112, Monroe, WA 98272; (360) 794-5488.

Sky Valley Chamber of Commerce, 320 Main St., P.O. Box 46, Sultan, WA 98294; (360) 793-0983.

Wenatchee Valley Chamber of Commerce, 300 S. Columbia, Wenatchee, WA 98807; (509) 662-2116; www.wenatchee.org.

SOUTHBOUND *ESCAPES*

SOUTHBOUND ESCAPE *One*
Washington's Southern Coast
NAVIGATING ALONG WASHINGTON'S WILLAPA BAY AND
CRANBERRY COAST / 3 NIGHTS

Sand dunes

Cranberry bogs

Sweeping ocean views

Columbia River boat traffic

Historic homes and forts

Marine museum

A getaway to Washington's south-ern coast includes a satisfying combination of beachcombing, kite flying, bird watching, and exploring some of Washington's earliest history. You'll cross the Willapa Valley, named after the First Nations Willapa people, who resided in this river dale that hugs the small unincorporated farming communities of Frances, Lebam, and Menlo. You'll wend your way to the coast along the Willapa River until you reach Willapa Bay, a region that provides 25 percent of the US oyster harvest. You'll navigate south along the bay, where the expansive Willapa National Wildlife Refuge and the sliver of Long Beach Peninsula is within your line of vision to the west. In days past, travelers on holiday used to take a narrow-gauge railway to the Long Island village of Ilwaco that even today retains a pleasantly old-fashioned atmosphere. On your third day, you will drive across the mighty Columbia to Astoria, Oregon. The town is a working port, where visitors and their children can easily while countless hours watching boat traffic entering and leaving the wide mouth of the river. As the oldest American settlement west of the Rockies, Astoria boasts many old and well-preserved homes, some of which are museums now.

DAY 1 / MORNING

Depart Seattle by way of I-5 south and continue to **Chehalis.** Before turning west onto SR 6, stop by the **Lewis County Historical Museum,** 599 NW Front Way (360-748-0831; www.lewiscounty museum.org). The museum houses intricate Chehalis tribe basketry, a Native American diorama, and a detailed model railroad depicting Lewis County. Continue west 3 miles on SR 6 to the **Claquoto Church,** 125 Water St., originally located in a now-defunct pioneer town of the same name, and later moved near Chehalis. The structure, an old Methodist church, is nicely modeled after a New England meeting house. Built in 1857, it is one of the oldest surviving Protestant churches in Washington.

As you drive west, consider stopping at the 840-acre **Rainbow Falls State Park,** situated in the heart of old-growth forest and framed by 3,400 feet of Chehalis River shoreline. Soon after, you will note the town of **Pe Ell,** its name said to reflect the attempts of local Native Americans to pronounce the name of Pierre Charles, an early French Canadian settler. The area once knew bustling commerce, primarily in lumber and sawmills. Near the town of Menlo is a pull-off with a wooden heritage marker noting the grave of Willie Keil, son of the religious leader William Keil. Nineteen-year-old Willie contracted malaria and died shortly afterward. Close by is **Raymond,** named after the town's first postmaster. Raymond is considered one of the most fertile tree-growing regions in the world.

The town serves as the gateway to the Willapa River and bay but may be most noteworthy for its numerous pieces of **Wildlife-Heritage Sculpture** that are on display along US 101 and on SR 6. This collection of steel heritage sculptures of loggers, Native Americans, bears, and shorebirds is a fine rendering of the area's history.

In Raymond you will find the one and only **Northwest Carriage Museum,** 314 Alder St. (360-942-4150; www.nwcarriagemuseum

.org), open Sept through Apr, Wed through Sat, 11 a.m. to 4 p.m. Numerous interactive exhibits are popular with children. Next door is the **Willapa Seaport Museum,** 310 Alder St. (360-942-4149; www.willapaseaport.org). The museum offers a detailed look at Raymond and South Bend's seafaring history. If you are in the area on a Friday or Saturday, May through Sept, drop by the **Willapa Public Market,** where you can pick up local produce, hand-crafted items, and more. Even today you can watch classic silent films at the **Raymond Theater,** 323½ 3rd St. (360-942-4127), which opened in 1928 with the silent feature *The Jazz Singer.* The building is listed on the National and State Registers of Historic Places. Locate the early logging scene mural at 5th and Blake Streets, a painting that, again, reflects a time when Raymond was bustling with logging commerce. Have lunch in Raymond.

LUNCH **Slater's Diner,** 124 7th St.; (360) 942-5109. A '50s diner that serves stuffed pocket-bread sandwiches, flavorful clam chowder, and criss-cross fries with ranch dressing.

AFTERNOON

You will pass the town of **South Bend** as you drive southwest on your way to US 101. Be sure to take a look at the incongruous **Pacific County Historical Courthouse,** 300 Memorial Dr., South Bend (www .co.pacific.wa.us/courthouse/historic.htm). Built in 1911, the palatial building has been dubbed "The Gilded Palace of Extravagance" because of the cost of construction. Planning dinner? Choose from a range of seafood in a live tank at **East Point Seafood Company,** 313 W. Robert Bush Dr. (360-665-6188; www.eastpointseafood.com). Closed Sun. Continue south on US 101 for approximately 25 miles to Ilwaco.

Now you're on SR 103, Long Island Peninsula, in the town of **Ilwaco,** a community that claims the title "Salmon Capital of the World." Here gill-netters and trappers fought ferociously over fishing grounds at the turn of the 20th century. Learn about Northwest heritage, from Native American Chinook life to the logging and fishing industries, at **Columbia Pacific Heritage Museum,** 115 SE Lake St. (360-642-3446). The museum's loop map (www.funbeach.com/wp-content/uploads/2010/08/LBPmap.pdf) will guide your scenic 3-mile trip around the southwestern tip of the peninsula. Outdoor murals grace the walls in Ilwaco and other peninsula towns; they all are part of a plan to attract visitors. Drive down to the harbor to see the busy tangle of boats and crab pots, charter fishing companies, canneries, and cafes, all mingling on the waterfront. The harbor has moorage for 1,000 boats. **Dockside Cannery and Gift Shop,** Port Of Ilwaco, 117 Howerton Way (360-642-8879), on the waterfront, sells fresh seafood and gift packs.

Stop at **North Head Lighthouse,** located just 2 miles north of Cape Disappointment (formerly Fort Canby State Park; www.parks.wa.gov), built in 1899 to warn boats approaching from the north. From this bluff above the Pacific you have a panoramic ocean view. The **Lewis and Clark Interpretive Center** (360-642-3029; www.parks.wa.gov/interp/lewisandclarkcenter), high on the cliffs of Cape Disappointment State Park, is open daily year-round. Stormy weather creates wild surf action as enormous breakers slam against steep cliffs below the interpretive center. Inside you can trace the intrepid explorers' adventures through pictorial displays, which include excerpts from their original journal entries. Ramps take you from the planning of the expedition in 1804 to its final destination here on the Pacific Ocean. Nearby **Waikiki Beach,** a local picnic favorite, is the only relatively safe swimming beach in the area. Drive to the Coast Guard station south of the interpretive center and walk the ¼-mile path to the 1856 **Cape**

Disappointment Lighthouse, one of the oldest lighthouses on the West Coast. Captain John Meares named Cape Disappointment in 1788, when he was unable to cross the rough Columbia bar. More than 200 ships have been wrecked or sunk in these treacherous waters.

Head north 2 miles to **Seaview,** once a fashionable resort town and noteworthy today as the home of historic Shelburne Inn, your lodging for the next 2 nights.

DINNER   **Shoalwater Restaurant** in the Shelburne Inn; (360) 642-4142; www.shoalwater.com. Gourmet dining emphasizing regional foods and fine wines. Candlelight, linens, stained glass, quiet atmosphere.

LODGING   **Shelburne Inn,** 4415 Pacific Way, at 45th Place, Seaview; (360) 642-2442 or (800) INN-1896. Fifteen rooms and 2 suites have quality antique furnishings; wardrobes, canopy beds, and armoires are all carefully chosen and stand against a backdrop of jewel-toned walls that accentuate different styles of wood molding.

DAY 2 / MORNING

BREAKFAST   Full country breakfast served family-style in the **Shelburne Inn;** complimentary for hotel guests; might include sourdough chocolate waffles, wild mushroom omelets with pesto cream sauce, or a lavish baked apple upside-down French toast.

Explore the Long Beach section of the **Willapa National Wildlife Refuge,** which has more than 15,000 acres of tidelands, rain-forest, ocean beaches, and tiny meandering streams, as well as several rare remnants of old-growth coastal cedar forest. This area offers parents a grand opportunity to show children what the Pacific

Northwest looked like 100 years ago. The Refuge diligently preserves this habitat for spawning wild salmon, migrating shorebirds, and threatened and endangered species such as the marbled murrelet. To reach the Refuge Headquarters, take US 101 north, ignoring a large brown sign that says Willapa National Wildlife Refuge. Wait until you are approximately 10 miles from Seaview, near mile marker 24. A boat ramp on the left side of the highway offers the best departure point for **Long Island,** the Pacific Coast's largest estuarine island, with 5,640 acres and a rare 274-acre remnant of old-growth lowland coastal forest. Many of the red cedar trees in this grove are over 900 years old! The rain-drenched forests on the island grow rapidly and are dense with salal, huckleberry, Western hemlock, and Sitka spruce. Hundreds of species of mushrooms and other fungus also grow here.

Now explore the northern stretch of **Long Beach Peninsula,** meandering along sand dunes, forest paths, and cranberry bogs. Washington state is one of the major cranberry producers in the United States, along with Oregon, Massachusetts, New Jersey, and Wisconsin. Visitors can begin a self-guided tour of the prolific bogs in Long Beach by calling or stopping by the **Pacific Coast Cranberry Research Foundation,** 2907 Pioneer Rd. (360-642-5553; www.cranberrymuseum.com). Also at this address is the **Cranberry Museum and Gift Shop,** 2907 Pioneer Rd. (360-642-5553; www.cranberrymuseum.com). Open daily from 10 a.m. to 5 p.m., Apr 1 through Jan 1. Admission is free.

Long Beach is a favorite spot for younger travelers, who love its go-kart track, moped rentals, and horseback riding, as well as the oddities and kitschy souvenirs of **Marsh's Free Museum,** 409 Pacific Ave. (360-642-2188). They also love to climb the whimsical wooden sculptures in the mini parks and to buy kites at **Above It All Kites,** 312 Pacific Blvd. (360-642-3541). Even adult children find they can spend an exhilarating hour holding a bright dragon, box kite, or bird and fly it on the wide, windy beach, said to be the longest (28 miles) in the world. At the **World Kite Museum,** 303 Sid Snyder Dr. (360-642-4020), visitors can learn about kites from around the globe, how they were developed, why they were used during wartime, and what they contributed to the development of airplanes. The museum is open daily. For a break, drop by **Long Beach Coffee Roasters,** 811 Pacific Ave. S (360-642-2334), to sip fresh-brewed coffee and check your e-mail on free Wi-Fi. The establishment roasts its coffees daily. Buy sweets at **Anna Lena's Quilt Shop,** 111 Bolstad Ave. E (360-642-8585). Anyone with a sweet tooth will have a tough time deciding which of 24 fudge flavors to purchase at Anna Lena's. Always on hand are chocolate, cranberry, praline, mint, and Butterfinger. Other flavors—lemon meringue, pumpkin, and Baby Ruth—rotate.

LUNCH   **Bailey's Bakery and Cafe,** 26910 Sandridge Rd., Nahcotta; (360) 665-4449; www.baileysbakerycafe.com/home.html. Makes its own breads for sandwiches and paninis, as well as homemade soups, salads, and breakfast pastries.

At **Briscoe Lake,** off SR 103, you'll see rare, majestic trumpeter swans, which migrate to peninsula lakes and Willapa Bay in December and January. Pass Klipsan Beach and Ocean Park, which have good beach access.

AFTERNOON

Travel northeast on SR 103 across the peninsula to **Oysterville.** Great sailing ships loaded with oysters sailed to San Francisco from this point during gold rush days in the mid-1800s, when oysters cost $1 apiece. The industry collapsed and the village faded, but the gracious old homes and the pretty church are on the National

Register of Historic Places. Pick up a walking-tour map at **Oysterville Church** and amble into the previous century. If you didn't explore the Long Beach section of the Willapa National Wildlife Refuge, another choice is to explore **Leadbetter Point State Park** by driving to Stackpole Road, at the peninsula's northern tip, a quiet world of sand dunes, beach grasses, and hiking trails. Thousands of shorebirds feed and rest on the tidal flats and salt marshes during their migrations. The dunes are closed to the public to protect the snowy plover during the April-to-August nesting season, but the rest of the park is open year-round.

DINNER   **The Depot Restaurant,** 1208 38th Place; (360) 642-7880; www.depotrestaurantdining.com. Recipient of many "best" awards: best oysters, best clam chowder, best burgers; consistently voted one of the state's best restaurants.

LODGING   Shelburne Inn.

DAY 3 / MORNING

BREAKFAST   Full country breakfast served family style in the **Shelburne Inn;** complimentary for hotel guests.

Drive south on US 101 and cross the **Astoria-Megler Bridge** over the Columbia River. The bridge stretches 4.1 miles across the mouth of the river from Point Ellice, Washington, to Astoria, Oregon, and is the longest "continuous truss" in the nation. Freighters and pleasure boats still ride the broad 1,000-mile-long Columbia River across that treacherous bar to the Pacific, which Native Americans' canoes and explorers' boats attempted without success in years gone by. The best places to watch maritime activity are at the **Maritime Memorial Park,** the sheltered viewing deck at 6th Street, or the 14th Street ferry dock, where visitors can read kiosks about the earliest days on the river.

In 1811 John Jacob Astor built his fur-trading post and the Fort Astoria stockade in this rain-washed, fish-rich, hilly corner of Oregon. Fishing, logging, and canning drew many Chinese, Swedish, Norwegian, and Finnish settlers. By 1900 **Astoria** was the largest city in the state. It's still a sizable fishing port, keenly aware of its historic position and honoring its Scandinavian heritage. In Astoria, give in to temptation at the **Home Bakery Company,** 2845 Marine Dr. (503-325-4631), an authentic Finnish bakery. Try the warm Danish pastries, maple bars, and doughnuts with a cup of coffee. Start your exploration on **Coxcomb Hill,** where a mural depicting historical highlights spirals up **Astoria Column.** Climb the 125-foot column's 166 steps for a sweeping view of the city, the long bridge, and the hills of Washington. Watch the Pacific Ocean meet the river in a roll of thunder. Tour a replica of the **Fort Astoria log stockade,** a National Historical Landmark, at 15th and Exchange Streets. Don't miss one of America's finest nautical displays at the ultramodern **Columbia River Maritime Museum,** 1792 Marine Dr. (503-325-2323). The museum exhibits historic sailing vessels, a river steamer wheelhouse, World War II submarine periscopes, and the historic West Coast lightship *Columbia.* Next stop is **Josephson's Smokehouse and Specialty Food,** 106 Marine Dr. (503-325-2190 or 800-772-FISH), where alder-smoked seafood is produced and shipped all over the world; there's none better.

LUNCH   **Drina Daisy,** 915 Commercial St., Astoria; (503) 338-2912; www.drinadaisy.com. Provides visitors and locals alike with the opportunity to sample the delectable dishes from Bosnia. The restaurant's chef worked for years in restaurants in Sarajevo. The menu features plenty of roasted lamb, pickled and fresh vegetables, and spinach and meat pies. If you can't get there for lunch, remember, there's always dinner.

AFTERNOON

Park at **Flavel House,** 441 8th St. (503-325-2203), an ornate 1883 Queen Anne mansion built for Captain George Flavel, a well-respected river pilot. It was saved when a 1922 fire burned much of the town, and the house now is a museum operated by the Clatsop County Historical Society. Buy a walking-tour map in the museum, and explore 70 other gracious old homes bearing historical markers. Browse a few shops along the way. Astoria also offers a small but satisfying number of art galleries for window shoppers. Among them are **Michael's Antiques,** 1004 Marine Dr. (503-325-9032), which features Asian and Victorian antiques plus the works of Pacific Northwest artists; **Pacific Rim Gallery,** 1 12th St. (503-325-5450); and **RiverSea Gallery,** 1160 Commercial St. (503-325-1270; www.riverseagallery.com/index.html). All of them showcase fine-quality craftsmanship. Choose your favorite historic clothing style at **Personal Vintage Clothing,** 100 10th St. (503-325-3837), which sells hats, beaded bags, jewelry, linens, and laces. Fine **Finn Ware,** 1116 Commercial St. (503-325-5720; www.finnware.com), sells distinctly Scandinavian crystal, pottery, jewelry, clothing, home decor, hand crafts, and more.

Drive 6 miles south on US 101 to **Fort Clatsop National Memorial** (503-861-2471 or 800-967-2283; www.nps.gov/lewi/planyourvisit/fortclatsop.htm). Explore a reproduction of the fort Lewis and Clark used for their expedition during the wet winter of 1805–06. Enjoy the center, its theaters, and interpretive displays by buckskin-clad rangers who tan hides, cure jerky, make candles, and carry muzzle-loaders just as the explorers used to do. Follow the coastal road to the northwestern tip of Oregon and **Fort Stevens State Park** (503-861-2471; www.oregonstateparks.org/park_179.php), a military reservation built during the Civil War to guard the river mouth from Confederate attack. It is now a 3,800-acre park with campgrounds, bicycle and hiking trails, beaches, and an interpretive center. The shipwrecked remains of the **Peter Iredale** have poked through the sand here since 1906. Artifacts from the ship are displayed in the **Clatsop County Heritage Museum,** 714 Exchange St. (503-325-2203; www.cumtux.org).

DINNER   **T Paul's Urban Cafe,** 1119 Commercial St., Astoria; (503) 338-5133; www.tpaulsurbancafe.com. An informal eatery that takes full advantage of the area's fresh seafood, in delicious tacos, quesadillas, pastas, and soups. Their substantial desserts are winners, too.

LODGING   **Britta's Inn Bed & Breakfast,** 1237 Kensington Ave., Astoria; (503) 325-4940; www.brittasinn.com. A lovely restored three-story 1914 Craftsman-style home. Breakfasts include juice, muffins, and entrees, always organic and based on seasonal ingredients. A full breakfast is included in the room rate at Britta's.

DAY 4 / MORNING

Return home, again crossing the Astoria-Megler Bridge over the Columbia to Washington. Take SR 401 north to SR 4 east to Longview, then take I-5 north to Seattle.

There's More . . . .

Art galleries. **Wade Gallery,** 223 Howerton Way, Ilwaco; (360) 642-2291. Specializes in photography of the Northwest.

    Wiegardt Studio Gallery, 2607 Bay Ave., Ocean Park; (360) 665-5976; http://ericwiegardt.com. Eric Wiegardt's watercolors, with their muted pastel colors, soothe the eye, while his vibrant acrylics excite. Many are based on local themes, making them a special and not unreasonably expensive souvenir from your coastal visit.

Boating. Bring your own boat to Long Beach Peninsula. Boat from Nahcotta to Long Island, in Willapa Bay, and hike up to the last known groves of old-growth cedar in the United States. Consult tide tables to avoid high tides.

Fishing. Tiki Charters, 350 Industry St., Astoria; (503) 325-7818; www.tikicharter.com. Offers high-quality fishing trips in Astoria. Salmon, tuna, and halibut fishing charters and crabbing trips available.

Golf. Peninsula Golf, 97th and SR 103, North Long Beach; (360) 642-2828; www.peninsulagolfcourse.com. Nine-hole course surrounded by old-growth pines and wildlife habitat. Open year-round.

Willapa Harbor Golf Course, 2424 Fowler St., Raymond; (360) 942-2392; www.willapaharborgolf.com. This 9-hole course is considered one of the most challenging and picturesque in southwest Washington.

Museums. Clatsop County Historical Society Heritage Museum, 714 Exchange St., Astoria; (503) 325-2203; www.cumtux.org. Housed inside Astoria's old neoclassical city hall. Exhibits include Native American baskets and tools from logging and fishing industries, both economic anchors in Astoria's early economy. A photography exhibit pays compassionate tribute to the region's diverse immigrant settlements.

Parks. Ray Spurrell Walkway, Raymond. Overlooking the docks and the Willapa River. Located adjacent to Robert Bush Park.

Willapa Landing Park, Eighth and Franklin, Raymond. This 12-acre park is located along the Willapa River and includes a wetland trail, boat launch, fishing pier, picnic tables, and interpretive displays.

Shopping. **Pacific Coast Antique Mall,** 1206 47th Place, Seaview; (360) 642-7199. Several dealers sell wares in a colorful old house.

Special Events . . . .

LATE APRIL
Astoria-Warrenton Crab and Seafood Festival, Astoria. Carnival, wine tastings, arts, crafts, Dungeness crab.

MAY THROUGH OCTOBER
Astoria Sunday Market, Astoria. Explore this robust street fair covering 4 blocks and selling innovative foods and fresh produce, as well as high-quality handmade gifts and souvenirs.

MAY
Blessing of the Fleet, Ilwaco. Children's parade, salmon barbecue, flowers strewn on the waters.

JUNE
Scandinavian Midsummer Festival, Astoria. Listen to traditional Scandinavian folk music and learn age-old dance steps; learn about Scandinavian cultures and sample Scandinavian cuisines.

Northwest Garlic Festival, Ocean Park. Crafts, music, and garlic-laced foods.

JULY
SandSations Sand Sculpture Contest, Long Beach. Cash prizes for winning sand sculptures.

Finnish American Folk Festival, Naselle. Biennial. Authentic Scandinavian music and food, plus photography exhibits. You can learn folk dancing, too.

AUGUST
Washington State International Kite Festival, Long Beach. Week-long celebration of kites with a kite-flying competition on the beach; one of the world's largest kite events.

SEPTEMBER
Rod Run to the End of the World, Ocean Beach. Classic-car and hot rod show with more than 1,000 participants.

DECEMBER
Fort Clatsop Living History, Astoria. Dramatic re-creations of the region's history located at this reproduction of Lewis and Clark's winter fort.

Other Recommended Restaurants and Lodging . . . .

ASTORIA
Astoria Inn, 3391 Irving Ave.; (503) 325-8153 or (800) 718-8153; www.astoriainnbb.com. An 1890 Victorian home located on a hillside, offering fabulous views of the harbor's changing panorama. Lavish breakfasts include fresh fruit and meats.

Hotel Elliott, 357 12th St.; (503) 325-2502 or (877) 378-1924; www.hotelelliott.com. In Astoria's downtown historic district. Thirty-two lovingly restored rooms and suites with heated-tile bathroom floors, cedar-lined closets, antique sleigh beds, and period furnishings. Views of the Columbia River or historic downtown from each room and from a 6th-floor roof garden. Complimentary breakfast.

Rose River Inn, 1510 Franklin Ave.; (888) 876-0028 or (503) 325-7175; www.roseriverinn.com. Just 3 blocks from Astoria's historic downtown. Provides a full breakfast in a dining room overlooking the Columbia River. Guests have access to free Wi-Fi.

SEAVIEW

42nd Street Cafe, 4201 Pacific Hwy.; (360) 642-2323; www.42ndstreetcafe.com. Serves gourmet comfort food, and numerous food publications seem to agree. Lunch might include beef or seafood burgers, cheese raviolis, clams, or a Caesar salmon salad. They also serve breakfast and dinner.

The Depot Restaurant, 1208 38th Place; (360) 642-7880; www.depotrestaurantdining.com. Located in an old train depot, this restaurant serves lamb, duck, seafood, and vegetarian entrees, all prepared with flair. It's best to make reservations.

Laurie's Breakfast Cafe, 4214 Pacific Way; (360) 642-7171. This tiny, lively establishment serves homemade biscuits and other satisfying breakfast items.

Lighthouse Oceanfront Resort, 12417 Pacific Way; (360) 642-3622 or (877) 220-7555; www.lighthouseresort.net. Families with dogs especially like this pet-friendly place. The resort features oceanfront townhouses and '50s-style 1- and 2-bedroom cabins, and easy beach access. Some townhouse rooms offer spectacular ocean views.

LONG BEACH

Boreas Bed & Breakfast Inn, 607 N. Ocean Beach Blvd.; (360) 642-8069 or (888) 642-8069; www.boreasinn.com. Hospitable innkeepers serve 3-course gourmet breakfasts and provide concierge services, if requested. Couples seeking a romantic getaway especially appreciate this place.

NAHCOTTA

The Ark, 273rd Street at the Nahcotta Docks; (360) 665-4133. Nationally acclaimed restaurant featuring regional seafood specialties, homemade breads, and fabulous desserts. Picturesque setting overlooking Willapa Bay. Hours vary seasonally; call first.

For More Information . . . .

Astoria-Warrenton Area Chamber of Commerce, 111 W. Marine Dr., P.O. Box 176, Astoria, OR 97103; (503) 325-6311 or (800) 875-6807; www.oldoregon.com.

Long Beach Peninsula Visitors Bureau, US 101, P.O. Box 562, Long Beach, WA 98631; (360) 642-2400 or (800) 451-2542; www.funbeach.com.

Willapa Harbor Chamber and Visitor Kiosk, P.O. Box 1249, South Bend, WA 98586; (360) 942-5419; www.willapaharbor.org/contact.php.

SOUTHBOUND ESCAPE *Two*
Columbia River Gorge
TRACING LEWIS AND CLARK'S COLUMBIA RIVER
JOURNEY / 2 NIGHTS

Your southern escape begins in Vancouver, Washington, an easy 2-hour drive from Seattle along I-5. With good restaurants, upscale boutique stores, and welcoming public spaces, Vancouver has much to offer visitors from the Seattle area.

> Basaltic cliffs
> Bonneville Dam
> Elegant resorts
> Fort Vancouver National Historic Site
> National Scenic Byway
> Walkable waterfront

Vancouver touts a 4-mile waterfront and more than 40 miles of walking trails. No doubt these are all reasons why Vancouver is ranked among *Money* magazine's "100 Best Places to Live."

The city is rich in history, too. Vancouver served as a fur-trading post for the Hudson's Bay Company 180 years ago, and the 366-acre Fort Vancouver National Site where trading and other commerce occurred is just east of downtown Vancouver. But even before the Hudson's Bay Company built Fort Vancouver, the Chinook Native Americans camped here, fishing for salmon and gathering roots and berries.

Leaving Vancouver, you will follow SR 14, a Scenic Byway known as the Lewis and Clark Trail. This route stretches from the Idaho border to the Pacific Ocean, winding through the scenic Skamania County. Just minutes east of Vancouver, the terrain becomes a naturalist's haven, as the route crosses the Cascades at sea level and closely hugs the river shore, keeping visitors in close contact with lovely panoramas.

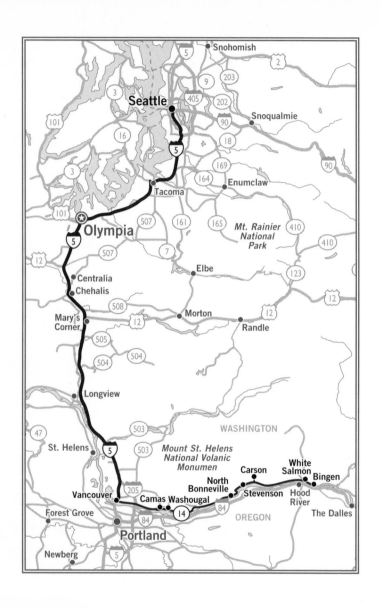

Enough sights dot the Washington Gorge landscape that children have plenty to explore, from the beach where Lewis and Clark's Corps of Discovery passed through in 1805 and 1806, and an upriver interpretive museum with hands-on petroglyph displays, to ladders at fish hatcheries that help the salmon and steelhead cross treacherous river barriers.

DAY 1 / MORNING

Begin at **Fort Vancouver National Historic Site** (www.nps.gov/fova), which opens at 9 a.m. From I-5, take the exit to Mill Plain Boulevard. Turn right onto Fort Vancouver Way and follow it to the roundabout; turn right and follow signs to the visitor center, where you can pick up a map.

In addition to a fur-trading center, the fort served as the region's first military post. Inside **Fort Vancouver**'s towering walls, you will learn about the different industries that supported this self-contained community: Bakers made hundreds of biscuits for the brigades and for trading at the bake house, and blacksmiths made iron and steel tools for the fur trade at the blacksmith shop. You also will see the jail, the fur warehouse, and the kitchen. Also at the site is the **Pearson Air Museum** (360-694-7026), open Wed through Fri. Hours vary seasonally, so call first. This museum is enormous, housing vintage and World War II aircraft. The **Pearson Field Historic Hangar,** one of the nation's oldest continually operating airfields, is also here.

Now drive to downtown Vancouver, where you will get your bearings at **Esther Short Park**, at West 6th and West 8th Streets and Esther and Columbia Streets, the oldest public square in the Pacific Northwest. Now the park is the heart of downtown Vancouver, with its 69-foot brick **Salmon Run Bell Tower** and glockenspiel diorama.

A gazebo, towering Douglas firs, walkways, a play structure, and several bronze sculptures, make the park a pleasant respite for sitting and gazing, too. The **Old Slocum House**, built in 1867 and the only remaining building from Vancouver's old residential neighborhood, is used for theater productions. **Vancouver Farmers Market**, open Sat and Sun in Mar at 6th and Esther Streets, has been selling local produce and crafts for more than 20 years.

Walk east, toward Main Street and the **Clark County Historical Museum**, 1511 Main St. (360-993-5679; www.cchmuseum.org). Open Tues through Sat, from 11 a.m. to 4 p.m., the museum is housed in a former Carnegie Library, built in 1909. The building is one of 2,509 libraries that 19th-century industrialist Andrew Carnegie built between 1883 and 1929. Now on the National Register of Historic Places, the museum houses a Native American gallery, a railroad exhibition, American military memorabilia, and artifacts dating back to the 13th century. Children enjoy the dioramas of an old country store, a country kitchen, and a doctor's office. From May through Sept, you can take a museum-sponsored historical walking tour as well.

Step outside and walk a few blocks to the **Old Town Antique Market**, 806 Main St. (360-750-9100), with 3 floors of antiques and collectibles. It is open everyday from 11 a.m. to 6 p.m.

LUNCH   The Rosemary Cafe, 1001 Main St.; (360) 737-7611. Child-friendly and wheelchair accessible. They serve veggie paninis, turkey avocado sandwiches, homemade soups, and a chicken salad locals say is addictive.

AFTERNOON

Leaving Vancouver, you will drive east on SR 14 for 14 miles to **Camas.** It takes only 20 minutes to reach Camas, where the carefully restored main street is lined with lush, plant-filled islands that slow traffic and greatly reduce street noise by several decibels. Old-fashioned cast-iron and wood benches, ceramic fountains, and bronze sculptures give the town a warm ambience. Small, upscale boutiques and pleasant restaurants offer visitors plenty of opportunities to window shop, and enjoy a few good meals.

Before dinner, browse shops such as **The Uncommon Gift**, 407 NE 4th Ave. (360-834-5445), just next door to the Camas Hotel. The shop sells attractive home-decorating merchandise and local art, such as hand-crafted jewelry. A block away, **Navidi's Olive Oils and Vinegars,** 322 NE Cedar St. (360-210-5921; www.navidioils .com), sells high-quality olive oils and vinegars from around the world.

Another option is to drive to the pretty **Lacamas Park**, covering 312 acres, for an evening stroll. Drive north on 6th Avenue and turn left on Garfield Street. Follow SR 500 West signs for 1.2 miles to Lacamas Park. There will be a parking lot on your right. Stay on the path by the lakeside, and you will be able to take a 1.6-mile walk around the lake.

DINNER   **Kop Chai**, 325 NE Cedar St., Camas; (360) 834-5287. They're just a block from your lodging and serve generous helpings of quality Thai food. Their fresh salad rolls, fried wonton, curries, and noodle dishes are made on-the-spot and are reasonably priced.

LODGING   **Camas Hotel**, 405 NE 4th Ave., Camas; (360) 834-5722; www.camashotel.com. This hotel has experienced a few transformations in its hundred-year history. The hotel's new owners have renovated the moderate-size rooms, all located on the second floor, to include Wi-Fi, mini-fridges, cheery, all-white tile bathrooms, hand-crafted furniture, and designer linens and toiletries. The hotel offers a basic self-serve continental breakfast with cereal and rolls in its sunny guest kitchen.

DAY 2 / MORNING

BREAKFAST Camas Hotel.

A few miles east on SR 14 is **Washougal**, Camas's sleepy neighbor, which draws its share of tourists with the **Pendleton Washougal Woolen Store**, 2 Pendleton Way (360-835-1118). The company offers tours of the mill daily. The store maintains a large selection of regular-priced and seconds woolen apparel for men and women, and its trademark Hudson's Bay striped woolen blankets and throws.

Across the street from the store is the **Two River Heritage Museum**, 1 Durgan St. (360-835-8742). The exhibits take a close-up look at the regional history.

East of Washougal is a must-see history stop, the 85-acre **Captain William Clark Park at Cottonwood Beach**. Meriwether Lewis and William Clark's Corps of Discovery stopped here in 1805 en route to the Pacific Ocean and on their return trip eastward in 1806. A handsome, natural bleached-wood arbor and a grove of cottonwood trees form the entryway to an easily accessible beach. As you walk toward the Columbia's waters, you will pass replicas of the dugout canoes the corps used to make its arduous 1,500-mile journey to the Pacific Ocean.

Back on SR 14, keep your eyes open for other historic sights along the way.

The **Historic Skamania General Store**, in **Skamania** on SR 14, sells food, gas, and more. Inside, the **Cook House Cafe**, 33001 SR 14 (509-427-4820), serves a country breakfast from 6 a.m. to 6 p.m. daily, in addition to homemade soups, sandwiches, and burgers.

Leaving Skamania, you will see **Beacon Rock State Park**, and an 848-foot projectile standing mighty against the elements. A steep 1.6-mile climb up the rock takes hikers to the core of what is an extinct volcano. Most outdoor books rate this hike "difficult," because of the steep ascent, but handrails do make the trek safe. Across the highway is a park with picnic facilities.

Near Skamania is **North Bonneville**, a town that moved to its current location in 1978. Yes, the town of North Bonneville literally had to move its entire infrastructure to accommodate the second set of power generators at Bonneville Dam. A visit to the gorge really isn't complete without a tour of **Bonneville Dam** (503-808-4515; www.nwp.usace.army.mil/op/b/home.asp), a project the US Army Corps of Engineers began during the Great Depression to generate power and to improve navigation on the river. The dam spans the Columbia River between Oregon and Washington. A sign on the right side of the highway announces the entrance to **Bonneville Lock and Dam Visitor Center**, where visitors can take either a guided or self-guided tour of both the newest and the oldest hydropower generating powerhouses on the Columbia River. The second floor of the visitor center provides a bird's-eye view of the generator rooms, dam, and fish ladders. In the **Fish Viewing Building**, children and adults alike marvel as they watch through underwater windows the adult salmon and steelhead climbing fish ladders to bypass the dam and continue up the river to spawn.

Downtown, you will see the trailhead for **North Bonneville Heritage Trails**, which lead to four different geographic areas in the community, including the fish-viewing area at Hamilton Creek, and the Pierce National Wildlife Refuge.

The **Bonneville Hot Springs Resort and Spa**, 1252 E. Cascade Dr., North Bonneville (866-459-1678; www.bonnevilleresort.com), shows a simple facade that masks the lodge's inner beauty. Visitors can schedule day retreats and access the mineral hot springs and a range of spa treatments, such as massages, manicures, facials, and body wraps. Call for prices. The dining room here is open to the public for lunch and dinner.

Continue 11 miles to **Stevenson**. Immediately after entering Stevenson city limits, turn left on Rock Creek Drive, and travel a short distance before turning left onto Skamania Lodge Way. Even visitors who aren't staying at **Skamania Lodge**, 1131 SW Skamania Lodge Way (509-427-7700; www.skamania.com), like to take a look at this elegant resort and spa on 175 forested acres. Although Skamania Lodge has 254 guest rooms and a huge lobby with a grand stone fireplace, the resort has managed to maintain an intimate feel. Despite the stylishness, the lodge's Cascade Room prepares meals that are tasty and reasonably priced. Its open to the public.

LUNCH　　**Skamania Lodge Cascade Room**, 1131 SW Skamania Lodge Way; (509) 427-7700. Overlooks an emerald-green golf course and a slice of the Columbia Gorge. The kitchen offers original takes on traditional lunch fare, such as the Chicken BLT, and also innovates with flatbread, such as one topped with smoked salmon, fresh mozzarella, and creamy spinach.

AFTERNOON

Just across the road from Skamania Lodge is the **Columbia Gorge Interpretive Center Museum**, 990 SW Rock Creek Dr. (800-991-2338; www.columbiagorge.org), owned by the Skamania County Historical Society and replacing the region's original small county museum. The displays highlight the gorge's natural and Native American history with a variety of baskets, stone tools, and beadwork. Hanging from the ceiling in the 2-story glass atrium is a 1917 Curtiss biplane. Several feet away is a Corliss steam engine, patented in 1849, and a 37-foot-high replica of a 19th-century fish wheel. Against the far wall, a Native American stands atop a 20-foot wood scaffold, preparing to catch salmon with a deep net of iron and wire, a method that many Native Americans still use.

Upstairs is the one-of-a-kind "World's Largest Rosary Collection," with prayer beads from around the world.

Up the road about 5 miles is **Carson**, where many summer travelers drive north on Wind River Highway, hoping for a view of the east side of **Mount St. Helens National Volcanic Monument**. If a diversion suits your fancy during summer travel, take the Wind River Highway, turning west on Curley Creek Road. There, the viewpoint—at least a hundred days during the year—provides unsurpassed views of the potentially volatile Mount St. Helens.

Continuing east on SR 14, you will drive through the tiny hamlets of Home Valley and Cook, en route to **Bingen**, a town that boasts an Amtrak train station and a large plywood mill. An old church is home to the **Gorge Heritage Museum**, 202 E. Humboldt St., which is open from mid-May to mid-Oct, Thurs through Sun, 11:30 a.m. to 4:30 p.m. A mercantile exhibit takes the visitor back to the time when merchants used scales to weigh goods, Victrolas were the primary source of family entertainment, and women of means wore silk dresses with elaborate embroidery or tatting.

Continue through Bingen, turning left on E. Jewett Boulevard and proceeding up the hill on SR 141 to tonight's lodging in the town of **White Salmon**, at the **Inn of the White Salmon**.

DINNER   **Henni's,** 120 E. Jewett Blvd., White Salmon; (509) 493-1555. Since the first night it opened in winter 2009, this restaurant has been busy, most likely because the owner and chef is well known among Columbia Gorge foodies on both sides of the river. They know his talent with gourmet comfort food, such as mac and cheese and chicken potpies, as well as unusual renditions of paella and pasta.

LODGING   **Inn of the White Salmon**, 172 W. Jewett Blvd., White Salmon; (509) 493-2335 or (800) 972-5226; www.innofthewhitesalmon.com. This 15-room inn has been hosting travelers since 1937. These days the inn especially attracts hikers, cross-country skiers, and kayakers, because of its proximity to Gifford Pinchot National Forest, Mount Adams Wilderness, White Salmon River, and as mentioned earlier, the east entrance to Mount St. Helens. Ask for one of the remodeled rooms, furnished simply and painted in soft colors.

DAY 3 / MORNING

BREAKFAST **Inn of the White Salmon**. In the morning you will find a substantial, self-service Scandinavian-style breakfast with wholesome cereals, breads, cold cuts, cheeses, and yogurt in a cheery breakfast room.

A half block from the inn is White Salmon's Bavarian-style City Hall with a clock tower, paying homage to the early German settlers of this region. Across the street is **White Salmon Glassworks**, 105 E. Jewett Blvd. (509-493-8400), featuring glasswork by local artists and a studio open to the public. **Artisan's Jewelry & Gallery**, 137 E. Jewett Blvd. (509-493-1333), open every day but Sunday, specializes in custom jewelry using diamonds, pearls, and precious gemstones; the gallery also sells pottery, paintings, and textiles.

Drive back to Seattle on SR 14 to I-5 north.

There's More . . . .

BINGEN

Brewery. **Bad Seed Cider House**, 415 W. Steuben St; (509) 493-3881; www.badseedcider.com. Open daily from 11 a.m. to 6 p.m. One of a dozen Northwest companies that specialize in hard-cider manufacturing.

LYLE

Winery. **Syncline Wine Cellars,** 111 Balch Rd., Lyle; (509) 365-4361; www.synclinewine.com. Open from Memorial Day until mid-Sept. They craft Rhône varietal wines here.

VANCOUVER

Cinema. One of the show-stopping attractions here is **Cinetopia**, 11700 SE 7th St. (360-213-2800), which they call the Northwest's first totally digital cinema. But there's much more, including leather seating, with some living-room theaters and private box seating, gourmet concessions, and a restaurant serving lunch and dinner inside the theaters.

Theater. **Magenta Theater**, 606 Main St.; (360) 635-4358; www.magentatheater.com. A nonprofit community theater that produces contemporary and classical works.

Walking and biking. The **Waterfront Renaissance Trail** is a 14-foot-wide, 14-mile paved trail connecting the waterfront with historical monuments to Vancouver's downtown. The trail frames a portion of a wildlife habitat and on clear days offers views of the snow-covered Mount Hood in Portland.

Special Events . . . .

MID-SEPTEMBER

48th annual Huckleberry Festival, Bingen. Brew fest, huckleberry pie, live music, kids' games, food, and arts and crafts booths.

Other Recommended Restaurants and Lodging . . . .

BINGEN

Solstice Wood Fire Cafe, 415 W. Steuben St.; (509) 493-4006; www.solsticewoodfirecafe.com. Open for lunch and dinner, specializes in wood-fired pizzas, grilled sandwiches, homemade soups, and salads with locally grown produce.

CAMAS

Around the Table, 316 NE Dallas St.; (360) 834-0171. Offers small-plate dining, ranging from appetizer-type plates of stuffed mushrooms and bacon-wrapped dates to braised beef short ribs and spiced pork tenderloin. If you plan your time right, you can enroll in one of their cooking classes.

Fairgate Inn, 2213 NW 23rd Ave.; (360) 834-0861; www.fairgate inn.com. Eight gracefully appointed suites, each with a unique selection of colors and furnishings, makes a stay at this inn celebratory. Full breakfasts are served in a pretty dining room.

Natalia's Cafe, 437 NE 4th Ave.; (360) 834-3421. Open for breakfast and serving lunch until 2:30 p.m. American cuisine features corned beef hash and homemade biscuits, and Russian cuisine includes blintzes and goulash.

CARSON

Carson Ridge Bed & Breakfast, 1261 Wind River Rd.; (509) 427-7777 or (877) 816-7908; www.carsonridgecabins.com. A filling buffet-style breakfast is served at 9 a.m., beginning with juice, fruit, and fresh breads, followed by a hot entree such as breakfast burritos, and a homemade fruit dessert. Each cabin has earthy furnishings and sophisticated amenities.

VANCOUVER

Cafe Al Dente, 907 Main St.; (360) 696-3463; www.cafealdente
.net/about.html. Diners here appreciate the hand-crafted pastas
and use of fresh local ingredients. The restaurant is open for lunch
and dinner, but hours vary, so call first.

Jerusalem Cafe, 106 E. Evergreen Blvd.; (360) 906-0306; www
.thejerusalemcafe.com. Diners can choose from a variety of pita
sandwiches with generous servings of chicken, lamb, or beef, as
well as lentil soup, roasted chicken, and shish kebab entrees. A
family member bakes a scrumptious baklava.

Julia Bakery, 2614 Fort Vancouver Way; (360) 993-0505; www
.juliabakery.net. A coffee shop with Wi-Fi, Julia's is said to be Vancouver's first artisan bread bakery. Besides bread, the bakery sells
scones, cakes, cookies, and pizzalike sandwiches. Stop here to
refuel before heading up SR 14.

Little Italy's Trattoria, 901 Washington St.; (360) 737-2363; www
.littleitalystrattoria.com. Crisp salads, pastas of all kinds, pizzas
and calzones, and authentic veal, lamb, and chicken entrees. Informal and a good place for kids.

For More Information . . . .

Greater Vancouver Chamber of Commerce, 1101 Broadway, Suite
100, Vancouver, WA 98660; (360) 694-2588; www.vancouverusa
.com.

Skamania County Chamber of Commerce, 167 NW 2nd Ave. (SR
14), Stevenson, WA 98648; (509) 427-8911 or (800) 989-9178;
www.skamaniachamber.com.

SOUTHBOUND ESCAPE *Three*

Mount St. Helens

EXPLORING THE VOLCANO / 1 NIGHT

Historic grist mill
Interpretive trails
Lilac gardens
Mount St. Helens National
Volcanic Monument
2,000-year-old cave
Accessible viewpoints of
volcanic landscape

Before May 18, 1980, **Mount St. Helens** was a pristine, symmetrical white peak, the queen of the Cascade Range. But mighty forces were brewing beneath that serene exterior. After 2 months of minor explosions and earthquakes, the mountain erupted in a blast of rock, ash, gas, and steam.

Within 10 minutes of the eruption, an immense plume of pumice and ash leaped 13.6 miles into the atmosphere and continued roaring upward for 9 hours. The volume of ash fall could have buried a football field to a depth of 150 miles. Mount St. Helens's height dropped from 9,677 feet to 8,363 feet, with a crater more than 2,000 feet deep.

When the summit and north flank collapsed in a giant landslide, a huge lateral blast blew sideways, obliterating or knocking down trees. Rock and melting ice created mudflows in the stream valleys, uprooting 150 square miles of trees and tearing out bridges and houses. The devastation left a landscape bleak and gray.

These days geologists say the probability of Mount St. Helens producing an eruption of debris or mudflow is relatively small. However, hikers need to exercise caution when crossing the gullies and streams draining the mountain, especially on the north side. Forest visitors near the volcano need to be prepared for potential ash fall. The US Forest Service routinely posts special conditions and closures on its website. Before visiting, travelers should either visit www.fs.fed

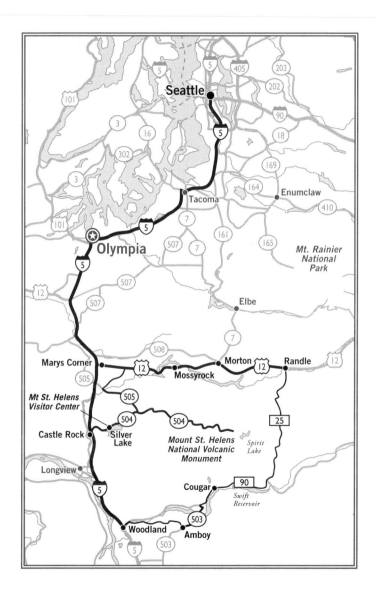

.us/gpnf/mshnvm or call (360) 274-0962 for changes in conditions. The east side of the mountain is open from Memorial Day until snow closes the roads in October, but you can still do a day trip up the west side of the mountain in winter. On the summer loop trip described here, you spend 1 day on the northwest side and the following day on the southwest side of Mount St. Helens. This tour touches the high-lights and will give you a sense of the awesome power that changed the structure of a mountain. As you walk, be careful of the fragile vegetation that is beginning to establish new life. Wear sturdy walk-ing shoes and bring water; there are few sources of water in the area.

DAY 1 / MORNING

Head south on I-5 to **Castle Rock**, Washington (exit 49). Drive 5 miles east on SR 504 to **Mount St. Helens Visitor Center**, 3029 Spirit Lake Hwy. (360-274-0962), a well-designed complex set in a wooded grove near the shore of **Silver Lake,** about 2 hours from Seattle. As national park budgets fluctuate, the center may be open only on certain days of the week, usually from 9 a.m. to 5 p.m. daily. The ongoing suggestion is to check for new times, phone numbers, events, and facilities. Trails (some paved and wheelchair accessible) extend from the center through the forest.

In the center you can obtain maps, information, and sightsee-ing suggestions from the helpful staff. Don't miss the theater pre-sentation, shown several times a day, that introduces the Mount St. Helens story. Exhibits explain the mountain's history of eruptions and graphically illustrate the 1980 devastation. You can even walk into the heart of the volcano—a replica that gives a simulated ver-sion of the mountain's interior.

Continue on SR 504 along the **North Fork of the Toutle River**. On the way you'll see an A-frame home that was half buried in the mudflow; you can walk through the dug-out rooms to see the effects of the disaster.

Stop for magnificent views at milepost 27, where Cowlitz County has opened the **Hoffstadt Bluffs Visitor Center** (360-274-7750). You can stand high above the Toutle River and look down the valley to the glistening gray flanks of Mount St. Helens. The center offers a few exhibits, but it is primarily an eating and shopping stop. Take a helicopter ride from here for a closer look at the mountain.

LUNCH **Fire Mountain Grill** at the Hoffstadt Bluffs Visitor Center, the only full-service eating establishment on the highway. A pleasant deck and marvelous views of Mount St. Helens make this spot worth a stop. Specialties are barbecued chicken and ribs, and smoked salmon corn chowder. Burgers, salads, and deli sandwiches round out the menu.

AFTERNOON

Continue east across the 370-foot-high, ½-mile-long bridge over **Hoffstadt Creek**. You are now in the blast zone, where there are views of Mount St. Helens along the way, but the next big view is from the **Charles W. Bingham Mount St. Helens Forest Learning Center** at milepost 33. This exhibit center, a joint project of the Washington State Department of Transportation and the Weyerhaeuser Company, was designed to show the destruction, recovery, and reforestation of the area. It tells the story from the point of view of the lumber industry. The Rocky Mountain Elk Foundation has joined this project to help provide views of the elk herds in the valley below the center.

Visit the **Coldwater Lake Recreation Area**. The lake formed when water from the Coldwater River backed up behind a natural dam created by a massive landslide after the 1980 eruption. Coldwater Lake has restrooms, a picnic area, paved interpretive trails, and a boat launch. Follow the ¼-mile **Winds of Change Interpretive Trail** to see how life has emerged from the ashes. Take the barrier-free **Birth of a Lake Trail** to the boardwalk over Coldwater Lake.

The very end of the road, just beyond the center, has been reserved for the **Johnston Ridge Observatory**, which is open from 10 a.m. to 6 p.m. May through Oct. You are now at an elevation of 4,500 feet, and just 5 miles from the volcano. There's a ½-mile walk on the eruption trail, where you can read about, and see for yourself, how the eruption shaped the landscape. Although the outdoor views are spellbinding, be sure to take some time for the indoor exhibits, which include live seismographs, and an excellent 16-minute film on the eruption.

If you are traveling during the summer and going on to the east side of the mountain, turn back on SR 504, turn north on I-5, and head east again on US 12 to **Marys Corner.** (Shortcut: Turn north off SR 504 before you get to Castle Rock and follow SR 505 through Toledo to Marys Corner.) One of the state's first homesteads, **Jackson House** (360-864-2643), is in this little community and occasionally open to the public.

In **Lewis and Clark State Park**, Marys Corner, you can walk in one of the last stands of old-growth forest along the Portland–Seattle corridor. Many of the Douglas fir, hemlock, and cedar trees are 500 years old.

Follow US 12 east to **Mossyrock**, a small town set in a beguiling valley of farms and rolling green hills. Wild blackberry vines arch over sagging wood fences along this road, and Queen Anne's lace grows tall against red barns. Acres of Christmas trees, tulip fields, and blueberries make the drive pass quickly. This is logging country, too, and you'll see hills shorn of trees.

East of town there's a view of **Mossyrock Dam**; at 606 feet, it's the highest dam in Washington. The dam created **Riffe Lake**, a

23-mile lake stocked with Coho and brown trout. Fishing, boating, and sailboarding are popular here.

Morton, a longtime logging town 31 miles east of Marys Corner, is famous for its annual rough-and-tumble logging show.

DINNER **Old Smokey's BBQ,** 31 E. Jackson St.; (309) 263-2509. A small, family-like atmosphere that serves up a variety of barbecue entrees: chicken, ribs, burgers, and sandwiches.

LODGING **Seasons Motel,** 200 Westlake Ave., Morton; (877) 496-6835; www.whitepasstravel.com/seasons. Offers clean, simple rooms with basic amenities. Serves a continental breakfast.

DAY 2 / MORNING

BREAKFAST Enjoy a full continental breakfast at the **Seasons Motel,** then explore a few sites in Morton.

East Lewis County Historical Museum, 710 Main St., Morton (360-496-6446), is also referred to as the "Old Settlers Museum," located in the home of Swedish immigrant Gust Backstrom. Showcasing old logging and mining equipment, the museum is open Sat and Sun, 1 to 4 p.m., Memorial Day through Labor Day.

It's 17 miles from Morton to **Randle**. Along the route you may spot hang gliders riding the wind currents on Dog Mountain. At Randle, turn south on FR 25.

In 9 miles you'll come to FR 26. Pass this road by, remaining on FR 25 for 11 miles until you reach FR 99. Turn west on the 2-lane, paved road. Starting in deep green forest, it leads into the blast area that appears to be one of abysmal destruction, but if you look closely, you'll see evidence of life's beginnings in the small plants.

Your first stop is at **Bear Meadow**, famous as the site where photographs were taken of the 1980 eruption as it occurred. Trails, picnic areas, and restrooms are in this area.

Nine miles in, at the junction of FR 99 and FR 26, you'll see the **Miner's Car**. The 1973 Grand Prix, resting atop downed trees, was hurled 50 feet during the eruption and then placed in its present location.

Meta Lake Trail 210 begins 100 yards west of Miner's Car, off FR 99. This is the only trail offering barrier-free access into the blast zone. A naturalist leads a walk and explains the changing environment, usually at mid-morning and again in mid-afternoon. Check the summer schedules for times and events. On the ⅛-mile, level paved path, you'll see small trees that survived the eruption, just 8½ miles away, because they were protected by snow and ice. Birds and insects have returned, and in **Meta Lake**, at the end of the trail, trout, salamanders, and frogs live once again.

Three miles from Meta Lake Trail, at **Independence Pass**, Trail 227 leads to striking views of the mountain, the crater with its growing lava dome, and **Spirit Lake**. Ascend to walk the ridge for ¼ mile, and you'll have views in all directions of the blown-down trees and acres of ash-covered slopes.

If you hike 1½ miles to a Spirit Lake overlook, you'll find interpretive signs pointing out the locations of buried campgrounds, Harry Truman's lodge, and cabins on the shores of the lake.

Spirit Lake, once a crystal-clear alpine gem, is regaining its blue clarity. The lateral blast was moving fast when it snapped off thousands of trees. The slower landslide sludge hit the lake and swooshed back uphill to wash the trees back into the basin. Many of those trees still float in the lake; others have sunk and are caught on the bottom, perhaps to become a future petrified forest. Farther on, the trail narrows and passes rock pinnacles, eventually joining **Norway Pass Trail**.

Walk Trail 227 back to FR 99, and drive deeper into the national monument; in 4 miles you'll reach the end of the road at **Windy Ridge Viewpoint**, which is as close as you can drive to the crater. A parking area is on the edge of the restricted zone, which can be entered only with a permit, but you can hike without a permit if you stay on the trail.

On one side you'll notice a sand-ladder trail against a slope. If you climb the stair-step path to the top of the hill, you'll have a good vantage point into the immense crater and devastated area.

Retrace your route back to FR 25, and turn south. Drive 25 miles to join FR 90 at **Swift Reservoir**, a long lake south of Mount St. Helens. The lake has a boat launch, picnic and camping grounds, and some tourist facilities. Take FR 90 to FR 83, turning north to drive 2 miles to the **Trail of Two Forests**, one of the park's best barrier-free trails for wheelchairs. One forest is an echo of the past; the other is of living, growing lodgepole pines.

An easy, ¼-mile-loop boardwalk (protecting the fragile mosses and plants growing on the lava) passes 2,000-year-old tree molds, formed when a lava flow consumed the forest that once stood here. Interpretive signs tell the tale of the two forests.

Next, take FR 8303 to **Ape Cave**, so called because it was discovered in 1951 by members of a club nicknamed the Mount St. Helens Apes. The cave, formed by an eruption 2,000 years ago, is 12,810 feet long—the longest lava tube in the continental United States. Lanterns and guided trips are usually available. Wear a jacket, carry 2 light sources, and wear sturdy shoes. It's 42 degrees Fahrenheit year-round.

Ape Cave has 2 routes to explore. The lower cave, ¾ mile long and fairly level, is easiest and has unique features such as a "lava ball" wedged in the ceiling. Allow an hour and 15 minutes for a round trip. The more challenging upper cave has large rock piles to climb and an 8-foot lava fall.

Back on FR 83, turn northeast and travel 9 miles to **Lahar Viewpoint**, which provides a look at the southeast side of the mountain. A short trail leads to an interpretive sign that describes the path of the lahar (mudflow).

Drive another ¾ mile past the parking lot to the **Muddy River**, and you'll notice the bright-colored stratigraphic bands on the stream bank. Debris racing down the channel of Shoestring Glacier sliced away the hill, revealing deposits from previous eruptions. The lower, bright yellow layer was deposited 8,000 to 13,000 years ago.

Return on FR 83 to FR 90 at the western shore of Swift Reservoir. This is one of three reservoirs created by dams on the **Lewis River**.

Drive 8 miles to the town of **Cougar,** on **Yale Reservoir**, a lake known for its outstanding Dolly Varden trout fishing.

LUNCH   **Cougar Bar & Grill,** 16849 Lewis River Rd., Cougar; (360) 238-5252. There aren't many lunch options in this rugged area, but fortunately the Cougar Bar & Grill doesn't leave visitors wishing for a lot more. Diners are satisfied with the careful preparation of simple burgers and fries cooked to perfection and served with a smile. If you still have room, order a slice of freshly made pie.

AFTERNOON

Drive SR 503 west for 23 miles along **Lake Merwin**'s northern shore, to **Woodland.** The visitor center here sells souvenirs and such gifts as emerald obsidianite, a gemlike stone made from heat-fused volcanic rock; the center also provides maps and useful travel information. From Woodland it's a 90-mile drive north on I-5 to Seattle.

There's More . . . .

Camping. **Cougar Park and Campground,** 17432 Lewis River Rd., Cougar; (360) 238-5224. Tents only. Swimming, boat launch, fishing.

Climbing. Climbing permits are required for travel above 4,800 feet, or the tree line, year-round. A fee of $22 is charged for each permit purchased between Apr 1 and Oct 31; permits are sold in advance online on a first-come, first-served basis. A number of trails in the Mount St. Helens National Volcanic Monument have also been closed, so call the Climbing Hotline at (360) 247-3961 or visit the Mount St. Helens National Volcanic Monument website, www.fs .fed.us/gpnf/recreation/mount-st-helens.

Historic Sites. **Hulda Klager Lilac Gardens,** 115 S. Pekin Rd., Woodland; (360) 225-8996. A national historic site with an 1880s Victorian house, a country garden, and a gift shop. It's open every day from 10 a.m. to 4 p.m. The lilacs, which come in all shapes and shades of purple, magenta, and pink, generally bloom from mid-Apr to mid-May, but check www.lilacgardens.com first to confirm the blooming schedule. Other unusual varieties of shrubs and flowers complete this gracious garden during the rest of the year.

Cedar Creek Grist Mill, in **Amboy,** 8 miles from Woodland; www.cedarcreekgristmill.com. To get there, turn left off SR 503 to Northwest Hayes Road, which becomes Grist Mill Road. The water-powered mill was built in 1876 for nearby residents to bring their grain for milling into flour or livestock grain.

Museums. **Chief Lelooska Living History Presentation**, 165 Merwin Village Rd., Ariel; (360) 225-9522. Colorful, evocative, educational programs on Northwest Coastal Indian culture. Ceremonial dances, masks, songs, stories. Native American art and artifacts displayed in Exhibit Hall.

Overlooks. **Hopkins Hill**, 4 miles west of Morton. The hill provides a commanding view of the Mount St. Helens crater and, often, a column of steam.

Special Events . . . .

MID-AUGUST
Loggers' Jubilee, Morton. Parades, carnival, arts and crafts, bed races, quilting exhibition, logging skills competition: tree fallers, logrollers, woodchoppers.

LATE OCTOBER
Annual Apple Pressing, Grist Creek Mill, Amboy. Watch dozens of volunteers turn 8,000 pounds of apples into cider.

Other Recommended Restaurants and Lodging . . . .

COUGAR
Monfort's Bed & Breakfast, 132 Cougar Loop Rd.; (360) 238-5229. Quiet, no-frills getaway serves continental breakfast of bagels and yogurt. Near Yale Lake and Ape Cave.

SALKUM
The Shepherd's Inn, 168 Autumn Heights Dr.; (360) 985-2434 or (800) 985-2434; www.theshepherdsinn.com. A secluded respite for birders, hikers, and daydreamers who just want to sit by a fish-filled pond and daydream.

TOUTLE

Eco Park Resort and Backwoods Cafe, 14000 Spirit Lake Hwy.; (360) 274-7007 or (877) 255-1980; www.ecoparkresort.com. Log cabins, yurts, and RV and tent sites give visitors numerous lodging options. On-site cafe serves breakfast, lunch, and dinner for large appetites, including loggers' stews and double-chocolate cheesecake.

For More Information . . . .

Mount St. Helens Visitor Center, 3029 Spirit Lake Hwy., Castle Rock, WA 98611; (360) 274-0962.

Mount St. Helens National Volcanic Monument, 42218 NE Yale Bridge Rd., Amboy, WA 98601; (360) 449-7800; www.fs.fed.us/gpnf /mshnvm. For road conditions visit www.fs.fed.us/gpnf/recreation /current-conditions/roads.shtml before attempting to drive into the national monument area.

SOUTHBOUND ESCAPE *Four*

Mount Rainier Loop

ENCIRCLING THE CASCADES' HIGHEST PEAKS /
1 NIGHT

Mount Rainier National Park
Old-growth forests
Massive glaciers
Scenic railroad rides
Fields of wildflowers
300 miles of hiking trails

The highest mountain in the Cascade Range can be seen for 200 miles when the weather is clear. **Mount Rainier**'s snowy bulk rises 14,411 feet, enticing climbers, hikers, and other lovers of the wilderness. Twenty-six massive glaciers hold an icy grip on the tallest volcanic mountain in the contiguous United States.

Old-growth forests encircle the mountain. Douglas fir, red cedar, and Western hemlock soar 200 feet above the moss-covered valley floors. Through those trees, more than 300 miles of trails meander, leading to wildflower-spangled meadows and clear ponds. Glacier-fed streams rush through every valley.

Rainier is moody, and its weather unpredictable. Rain and snow may suddenly appear on a mild spring day and retreat as quickly. Glimpsed even through the clouds, the mountain is beautiful. Under sunny skies, Rainier appears in all its dazzling glory and is magnificent.

Much of the route outlined here is open only in summer. Always check the road status page first at www.nps.gov/mora/planyourvisit/directions.htm before leaving for Mount Rainier.

DAY 1 / MORNING

Mount Rainier is a 3-hour drive southeast of Seattle. The southwest corner of the park (Nisqually, Longmire, and Paradise) is open

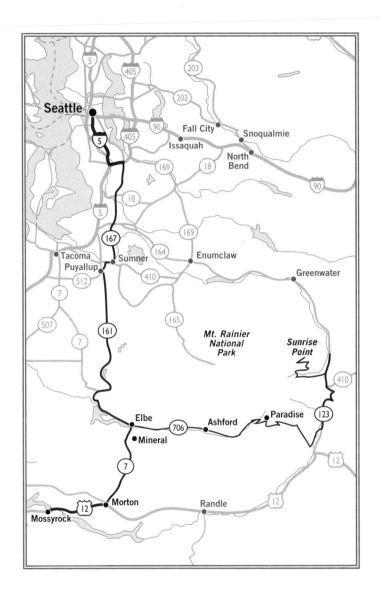

year-round. From Seattle, drive south on I-5 to I-405. Continue east on I-405 to SR 167. Turn south on SR 167 to SR 512 to SR 161, then east on SR 706 through Ashford to the Nisqually entrance. In this portion of the park, trails lead from the visitor center through the fragile, subalpine vegetation to ever-higher and more breathtaking views of glaciers and rocky crags.

The northeastern section of the park, SR 410 to Sunrise and White River, at the park junction, is closed for the winter from mid-October or earlier, depending on the first heavy snowfall. When the roads are clear in the spring, follow SR 410 to **Sunrise Point.** From here, the summit's crater rim and **Emmons Glacier**, 4 ½ miles long, are clearly visible. Mount Adams lies to the south, and Mount Baker protrudes on the northern horizon.

LUNCH   Picnic at **Sunrise Point**.

AFTERNOON

Follow SR 410 south to **Cayuse Pass** (4,694 feet), and veer left toward **Chinook Pass** (5,430 feet). Drive 3 miles for a striking view of Mount Rainier's east side.

Return to Cayuse Pass and take SR 123 south. Near the **Stevens Canyon** entrance, at the southeastern end of the national park, watch for signs to the **Grove of the Patriarchs.** Walk the 1-mile trail, crossing the **Ohanapecosh River** on a footbridge, to an island where you'll be in the midst of an ancient forest. The princely trees that grow on the island—Douglas fir, western red cedar, and Western hemlock—are 1,000 years old.

Drive the Stevens Canyon road west to **Paradise**. The road angles through thick forest, across rivers and creeks, rounding the bend at **Backbone Ridge** and heading north to **Box Canyon.** Through this narrow canyon, scoured by glaciers and carved by water, runs the Muddy Fork of the Cowlitz River.

Traveling west from Box Canyon, you'll see Stevens Ridge looming high on the right, with Stevens Creek below. In the fall the vine maples in this U-shaped valley blaze with color.

As the road twists toward the southern shores of Louise and Reflection Lakes, at the base of the **Tatoosh Peaks,** you'll see the three most prominent peaks, Stevens, Unicorn, and Pinnacle, thrusting sharply skyward, dramatically punctuating the rugged landscape.

When you reach Paradise Valley Road, turn right and climb upward until you arrive at last in Paradise. **Nisqually Glacier** and **Wilson Glacier** hang above, with Rainier's peak capping the view. At the new **Henry M. Jackson Memorial Visitors' Center** (360-569-6036), pick up maps and trail information. The center offers slide and film programs on Rainier and the park's history, as well as 360-degree views of the awe-inspiring surroundings.

During July and August the slopes of **Paradise Park** become tapestries of color and beauty, as delicate subalpine flowers bloom by the thousands. Trails wind through the meadows and over trickling brooks, luring you to explore.

Head out on your own or join one of the naturalist-led walks that begin at the visitor center. An easy 1-hour **Paradise View Glacier** walk exploring the flower fields starts at 2 p.m. Several other educational programs are available in the Paradise area during the day; it's helpful to view the park's website to plan before you leave home: www.nps.gov/mora/planyourvisit/paradise.htm.

Take **Skyline Trail** to **Panorama Point** for a comfortable, half-day, 5-mile hike replete with grand vistas. Marmots whistle and streams sing in the crisp, clear mountain air. A side trail crosses snowfields to end at **Ice Caves**, remnants of the once-immense caves carved by water flowing under glaciers.

DINNER **Paradise Inn Dining Room**, Mount Rainier National Park; (360) 569-2275. Grilled salmon, steak, and chicken, served in the dining room of a grand old lodge.

At 5:30 p.m. meet a park naturalist in the lobby for a 1-hour evening stroll in the valley. It's an excellent opportunity to take photographs and observe wildlife.

At 9 p.m. interpreters give slide-illustrated talks in the lodge lobby. Topics vary: Meadow ecology, volcanic geology, human effects on the mountain, and Native American views are a few.

LODGING **Paradise Inn**, Mount Rainier National Park. Open May through Oct. Imposing, 121-room lodge of Alaskan cedar. Simple rooms; some share baths. The views are incomparable. For reservations (a must), contact Mount Rainier Guest Services, 55106 Kemahan Rd. E, P.O. Box 108, Ashford, WA 98304; (360) 569-2275 for reservations only.

DAY 2 / MORNING

Rise at dawn for an early hike, if the weather is clear. There are few sights more exhilarating than Rainier's rosy-hued glaciers under the first rays of the morning sun.

BREAKFAST **Paradise Inn**. Standard breakfast menu, lavish Sunday brunch.

Head south from Paradise Park to the small community of **Longmire,** and stop for a tour of the second-oldest national park museum in the country. Open daily from 9 a.m. to 4:30 p.m., the small **Longmire Museum** (360-569-2211) offers exhibits that cover Rainier's geology, wildlife, and history.

As you drive west toward the Nisqually entrance, 6.2 miles from Longmire, the high branches of trees 600 to 800 years old will provide a billowy canopy over your car.

From the park's entrance, continue west on SR 706, along the banks of the Nisqually River. You might want to enjoy a meal in **Ashford** at the **Coppercreek Inn** (360-569-2326), which serves pancakes and French toast with its own blackberry syrup for breakfast, and chowders, stews, and chili for lunch. A baron built the inn, which is constructed of close-grained logs and features broad Dutch doors and a stone fireplace. After dining, drive and follow the signs to **Mount Rainier Scenic Railroad,** located south on SR 7, 54124 Mountain Hwy. E, Elbe (888-783-2611; www.mrsr.com). The old-fashioned train takes visitors on a 14-mile ride daily, from Memorial Day through Oct, and twice daily in Nov and Dec. Behind a vintage steam engine, open cars chug, steam, and whistle across high bridges and through deep forest to **Mineral Lake**. The train ride takes 90 minutes. The dinner train ride on Sunday lasts 4 hours.

From Mineral Lake continue south on SR 7 to Morton and US 12 to Mossyrock. Consider a stop just west of Mossyrock at the **DeGoede Bulb Farm and Gardens** and gift shop. Hours vary seasonally, so it's best to call (360-983-9000; www.degoedebulb.com). Follow US 12 to I-5 and head north to Seattle.

There's More . . . .

Hiking. **Naches Loop Trail**, near Chinook Pass and Tipsoo Lake (off SR 410, on the eastern border of the national park), is enchanting, with its subalpine firs and mountain hemlock trees, wooden bridge, and summer wildflowers. The trail connects with the Pacific Crest Trail, which extends from Mexico to Canada.

Silver Falls Trail, above Laughingwater Creek on the Ohanapecosh River, is a 3-mile loop trip from Ohanapecosh Campground,

2 miles south of the Stevens Canyon junction on SR 123. The trail leads to an 80-foot cascade of water so clear it has a silver cast. The vibrant green of the ferns and mosses in the Silver Falls gorge is stunning on a cloudy day.

Trail of the Shadows is a ½-mile trail through old-growth forest. Along the trail are signs that tell the story of James Longmire, a pioneer who built a resort and spa after he discovered bubbling mineral springs in the 1880s. Some of the springs are still surrounded by Longmire's original stonework enclosures, and one of his cabins is still on the property. The trail begins across the road from the Longmire Museum.

Mountain climbing. Climbing Rainier demands skill and experience. One-day seminars and equipment rentals are available from **Rainier Mountaineering Inc**. in Ashford (888-892-5462; summer only). They have exclusive rights to conduct guided climbs of the mountains. Winter address: P.O. Box Q, Ashford, WA 98304.

Skiing. **Camp Muir snowfield.** Gentle slope, snow-covered all year, on Mount Rainier's south side. No lifts. Hike up and ski down.

Crystal Mountain, 33914 Crystal Mountain Blvd., Crystal Mountain; (360) 663-3050; www.skicrystal.com. The largest ski area in Washington, and at 7,000 feet, it's Washington's highest. Located on the northeast section of Mount Rainier National Park. Has 2,600 acres with 11 chair lifts that transport skiers to 6 mountain peaks offering spectacular views on top.

Reflection Lakes. Safe cross-country trail skiing, easy access, and scenic grandeur. Camping allowed when snowpack is 3 feet deep. Park at Narada Falls, near Paradise.

Other Recommended Restaurants and Lodging . . . .

ASHFORD

Alexander's Country Inn, just outside Mount Rainier Park, 37515 SR 706 E; (360) 569-2300 or, within Washington, (800) 654-7615; www.alexanderscountryinn.com. Landmark country restaurant and inn with 12 rooms. Fresh fish entrees and memorable blackberry pie.

Rainier Overland Restaurant and Lodge, 31811 SR 706 E; (360) 569-0851 or (800) 582-8984; www.rainieroverland.net. Located 1 mile east of Ashford and 5 miles west of the southwest Nisqually entrance of Mount Rainier National Park. The motel and cabins are available year-round, with rooms for up to 4 people and cabins for 8. The restaurant menu features poultry and seafood entrees, salads, and sandwiches. Open daily Memorial Day through Labor Day. Breakfast and lunch also are available.

CRYSTAL MOUNTAIN

Crystal Mountain Hotels, 33818 Crystal Mountain Blvd.; (360) 663-2262 or (888) SKI-6400; www.crystalhotels.com. Crystal Mountain Hotels offers full-service mountain lodge facilities in 2 separate buildings: The Alpine Inn is traditional Bavarian-style; the Village Inn is more contemporary.

LONGMIRE

National Park Inn. Historic cedar lodge remodeled in 1989–90. Rustic and woodsy, with 25 rooms (2 are wheelchair accessible) and a view across Longmire Meadow to the mountain's peak. The only lodge in the park open all year. Reservations: Mount Rainier Guest Services, P.O. Box 108, Ashford, WA 98304-0108; (360) 569-2275; www.mtrainierguestservices.com/accommodations/national-park-inn.

White River Campground, Mount Rainier National Park; (360) 569-2211; www.nps.gov/mora/planyourvisit/campground-fees-and-reservations.htm. Keep an eye out for mountain goats near this campground (accessed from the White River entrance) on Mount Rainier. Insider tip: For wildflowers, hike 3 miles to Glacier Basin or 4.2 miles up, up, up to Summerland via the Wonderland Trail. No reservations (first-come, first-serve).

PACKWOOD

Inn of Packwood, 3032 US 12; (877) 496-6666; www.innofpack wood.com. Thirty-four older but very clean rooms. Nice views of Mount Rainier from window.

For More Information . . . .

Mount Rainier National Park, 55210 238th Ave. E., Ashford, WA 98304; (360) 569-2211; www.nps.gov/mora; also the official Mount Rainier website, www.visitrainier.com.

WESTBOUND *ESCAPES*

WESTBOUND ESCAPE *One*
Gig Harbor and Tacoma
DISCOVERING WATERFRONT VILLAGES AND
GLASS BRIDGES / 1 NIGHT

Boating
Glass museum
Pastoral country roads
Point Defiance Park
Seattle skyline
Waterfront villages

This is a short but sweet getaway near home. Gig Harbor, a historic maritime town 50 miles south of Seattle, was an isolated fishing village until a bridge was built in 1940. It's still a fishing village, where you can walk along the harbor and hear the boats gently bobbing on the water. But the town has quietly revamped its image, too, with upscale shopping and dining. The same is true of Tacoma. The city has long been the home of 700-acre Point Defiance Park—the Pacific Northwest's only combined zoo and aquarium that offers unforgettable views of Puget Sound, Mount Rainier, and the Cascade Mountains. Today's Tacoma offers much more. Its Museum District touts top-notch museums and even flaunts one that holds the world's largest private collection of valuable documents and manuscripts.

DAY 1 / MORNING

Leave Seattle on I-5 south and drive to Fauntleroy Cove, where the Washington State Ferries terminal is located. Take the ferry across Puget Sound to Southworth. Drive to SR 160 west, and then take SR 16 to Gig Harbor. Get your historical bearings by taking a self-guided tour; pick up a free History Walk brochure. You can expect to spend most of your day on Harborview Drive, the 2-mile

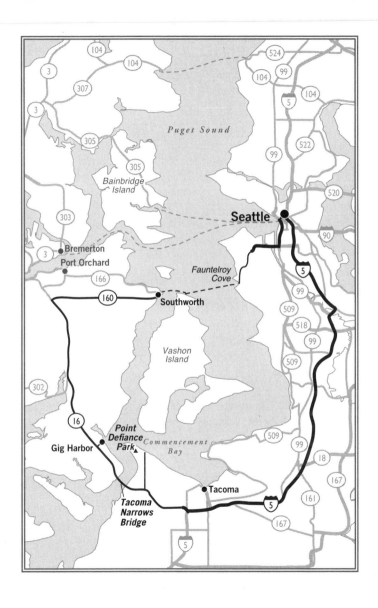

waterfront in the historic downtown district. The **Gig Harbor Visitor Information Center,** 3125 Judson St. (closed Tuesday), and most of the shops along Harborview carry copies.

For an in-depth historical overview, stop by the **Gig Harbor Peninsula Historical Society & Museum,** 4218 Harborview Dr. (253-858-6722; www.harborhistorymuseum.org). The new museum has a gallery dedicated to Gig Harbor's first residents, the Gig Harbor Band of the Puyallup tribe. A maritime gallery showcases the 65-foot fishing vessel *Shenandoah.* Also on site is the reconstructed **Midway School,** built in 1893. The gift shop includes children's books, Gig Harbor memorabilia, and work by local artists. Get the topographic picture of Gig Harbor by ascending 88 stairs on the Finholm View Climb, located on the waterfront at the head of the bay. The panoramic view of the town, with Puget Sound and Mount Rainier as a backdrop, will show you just how multifaceted Gig Harbor is.

Shopping in Gig Harbor is easy, because it's so accessible. You will find more shops than you can possibly browse through on this trip. A few you might be glad you visited: **Animal Crackers,** 3026 Harborview Dr. (253-858-1795; www.anicrackers.com), specializing in children's toys and maternity items. Kids immediately gravitate toward the corner where they can settle into furniture made just for little people, and watch a kid's movie. **Gig Harbor Gift Mall,** with 15 shops in one location, 3110 Harborview Dr. (253-851-7722; www.gigharborgiftmall.com), has antiques, nautical appliances, quilts, pillows, and much more. **Kit Kuhn, A Jeweler Designed for You,** 3104 Harborview Dr. (253-851-5546; www.kitkuhn.com), sells work so exquisite that a look around here is much like a visit to an art gallery. **Mostly Books,** 3126 Harborview Dr. (253-851-3219; www.mostlybooks.com), is just that, selling the latest best sellers and nonfiction, as well as a large selection of local, regional, and nautical books and maps, and titles to intrigue children. **Seaglass Interiors,** 3115 Harborview #B, (253-858-7184), sells classy marine-inspired items, such as sea-food-eating kits, and pillows, tableware, and pottery covered with ocean-inspired motifs of seashells, starfish, fish, and seabirds. If you happen to be in Gig Harbor on a Wednesday, stop by the **Gig Harbor Farmers Market** down on the waterfront to browse, mingle, and purchase a delicious, inexpensive lunch. The market also is open on Saturday on Kimble Drive, just off SR 16. You won't miss the locations. Just follow the fragrance of grilled Polish sausages, homemade fruit pies, and fresh-brewed coffee.

LUNCH **Anthony's at Gig Harbor,** 8827 N. Harborview; (253) 853-6353; www.anthonys.com/restaurants/info/gigharbor.html, across from the Finholm View Climb. Promises lovely views of the harbor and the freshest of seafood entrees, although for lunch you may just opt for the award-winning clam chowder. If it's the weekend and you haven't had breakfast yet, drop by a favorite local hangout, the **Tides Tavern,** 2925 Harborview; (253) 858-3982; www.tidestavern.com, at the harbor's south end. Like many other Gig Harbor businesses, the tavern occupies a building that has been on the harbor since 1910, just alongside the public ferry landing. Besides the standard egg-and-potatoes fare, the tavern serves breakfast pizzas, breakfast sandwiches, and a tasty crab croissant.

AFTERNOON

From Gig Harbor, take SR 16 southeast to **Tacoma Narrows Bridge,** a pair of suspension bridges that will take you across the Tacoma Narrows strait of Puget Sound between Gig Harbor and Tacoma city. The structure is the fifth-largest suspension bridge in the United States. The previous bridge, affectionately named Galloping Gertie, collapsed in 1940. Fortunately, no one died in the incident. Now take SR 163 north to **Point Defiance Zoo and**

Aquarium (253-591-5337; www.pdza.org). The zoo is more than 100 years old, and not only houses an incredible variety of animals but also stands in a truly lovely setting, with views of the Puget Sound and surrounding mountain ranges. Walk through a rain forest with Sumatran tigers, gibbons, and clouded leopards. Traipse along rocky shores to view walruses, sea otters, and puffins. Experience polar bears, foxes, and reindeer in an Arctic tundra. History buffs will want to see **Fort Nisqually Living History Museum,** where volunteers and staff in period clothing demonstrate 19th-century crafts. The museum is located in **Point Defiance Park,** 5400 N. Pearl St. (253-591-5339; www.fortnisqually.org), amid 700 acres of woodland trails, gardens, and waterfront views.

Unless you extend your stay, you won't be able to see all of Tacoma's museums, but you can select a couple in the Museum District, which includes the **Washington State History Museum,** 1911 Pacific Ave. (888-238-4373; www.washingtonhistory.org), displaying a pictorial history of the region's early settlers and the enterprises they developed, and the **Tacoma Art Museum,** 1701 Pacific Ave. (253-272-4258; www.tacomaartmuseum.org), with its fine collection of work from Northwest artists. The magnificent **Museum of Glass,** 1801 Dock St. (866-468-7386; www.museum ofglass.org) is as exquisite on the outside as it is on the inside. Leading to the museum is the The **Chihuly Bridge of Glass** (www .chihuly.com), a phenomenal 500-foot pedestrian bridge that links the Museum of Glass and Thea Foss Waterway. Inside you not only can view contemporary glass art but also watch resident glassblowers at work. Close to the Museum District is the **Tacoma Glassblowing Studio,** 114 S. 23rd St. (253-383-3499; www.tacoma glassblowing.com). The studio exhibits and sells the work of local glass artists in its gift shop. **Karpeles Manuscript Museum,** 407 S. G St. (253-383-2575; www.rain.org/~karpeles), about 1½ miles north, is the world's largest private library of valuable documents and manuscripts. You will find an original draft of the US Bill of Rights and *Webster's Dictionary* here.

DINNER   **Asado Cicina Argentina,** 2810 6th Ave.; (253) 272-7770; www.asadotacoma.com. Respected for its tasty appetizers at happy hour, delivered by friendly waitstaff. Open for lunch and dinner. Offering healthy fare: a variety of skewered meats, chicken entrees, and authentic South American seafood dishes.

LODGING   **Thornewood Castle Inn and Gardens,** 8601 N. Thorne Lane SW; (253) 584-4393; www.thornewoodcastle.com. It's a castle for sure, and perhaps a rare opportunity for you to stay in one. Luxuriate in the home's expanse and breathe the fragrance of the sunken English gardens. Although it was built in the Northwest "only" 100 years ago, many of its materials were extracted from a 400-year-old Elizabethan manor.

DAY 2 / MORNING

BREAKFAST   **Thornewood Castle Inn and Gardens.** If you are lucky, you will dine on the inn's signature Decadent French Toast, but hot entrees of egg casseroles and meats are equally indulgent and always accompanied by fresh fruit, breakfast pastries, and juices. The establishment gladly delivers breakfast to your room, but many don't want to miss indulging themselves in the opulent dining room.

It's likely that you have not seen all that you want to see in this small city. But try to see the old **Tacoma Union Station,** 1717 Pacific Ave. (253-863-5173; www.unionstationrotunda.org), the historic and architectural focal point on Pacific Avenue. With its broad, elegant rotunda, the building is an example of the Beaux Arts neoclassical style that includes strict symmetry, rounded arches, and an elaborately embellished copper dome. The station also contains Dale Chihuly's glass art.

There are numerous other neighborhoods in Tacoma that are worth a look: The **Dome District** (www.domebusinessdistrict.com) is not just the hub of the city's transportation line. It has plenty of shopping and dining opportunities, too. The neighborhood of **Fern Hill** (www.fernhillbusinessdistrict.com) marks the location of Washington's first road, where the Pony Express used to stop. Some of Tacoma's oldest buildings are here, including the **Fern Hill Methodist Episcopal Church,** built in the 1890s, and the **Fern Hill School,** which dates back to 1888.

For your short return trip home, leave Tacoma by taking the I-5 exit north to Seattle.

There's More . . . .

GIG HARBOR
Art galleries. **Water's Edge Gallery & Framery Inc.,** 7808 Pioneer Way; (253) 858-7449; www.watersedgegallery.com. Carries the work of local and regional artists in several media. Nice inventory of frames, prints, and posters.

Golf. **Chambers Bay Golf Course,** 6320 Grandview Dr., West University Place; (253) 460-4653 or (877) 295-4657. Offers wonderful views of Puget Sound. Will be the home of the 2015 US Open.

TACOMA
Art galleries. **Curtwright & Son Tribal Art,** 708 Market St., Suite 408; (253) 383-2969; www.curtwrightandson.com. The Northwest's oldest gallery since 1889.

Foss Waterway Seaport, 705 Dock St.; (253) 272-2750; www.fosswaterwayseaport.org. These maritime exhibits breathe life into Tacoma's waterfront history.

Museums. **Children's Museum of Tacoma,** 936 Broadway; (253) 627-6031; www.childrensmuseumoftacoma.org. The many stimulating hands-on exhibits are a welcome release for those who might have boundless energy.

Job Carr Cabin Museum, 2350 N. 30th St.; (253) 627-5405; www.jobcarrmuseum.org. Commemorates the first nonnative settler in the Tacoma area. Open Wed through Sat.

LeMay—America's Car Museum, 325 152nd St. E; (253) 536-2885 or (877) 902-8490; www.lemaymuseum.org. Recognized in the Guinness World Records as the largest privately held car collection in the world.

W. W. Seymour Botanical Conservatory, 316 S. G St.; (253) 591-5330; www.metroparkstacoma.org. No matter when you visit, there is always something in bloom in the 18th-century Victorian-style conservatory that's a permanent home to exotic tropical plants.

Shopping. **Home of Almond Roca, the Tacoma Factory Outlet,** 110 E. 26th St.; (253) 620-3067; www.brown-haley.com/ourstory.php. Established in 1927. Located in a small circular outlet store next to the Almond Roca Factory in downtown Tacoma. Open daily.

Special Events . . . .

JUNE

Maritime Gig Festival, Skansie Park, Gig Harbor. Several road race events, including one for kids, plus blues band performances, children's puppet theater, historic boat displays, and lots of food vendors.

SUMMER

Gig Harbor Art Walk. Every Thurs night in the summer. Some consider these the best small-town art walks in the Northwest, where participants can meet gallery owners and artists.

JULY

Two-day Ethnic Fest, Wright Park, Tacoma. The city has sponsored this event for 25 years to honor its diverse cultural and ethnic history. Reggae music, Celtic dancing, and Brazilian drum and dance are among the many performances that celebrate the region's mix of peoples.

AUGUST

Northwest Native Arts Market and Festival, Tacoma. At this event, visitors will find a juried art exhibition of Northwest Native American works. Other events include Native dance and vocal performances.

OCTOBER

Heineken City Arts Fest, Tacoma. Here's a music festival well-known for cutting-edge performances by a wide range of musicians, who belt out Scottish indie rock, gypsy punk, and hip-hop.

DECEMBER

Zoolights, Point Defiance Zoo and Aquarium, Tacoma. More than a half million colored lights make an already marvelous zoo dazzle after dusk. Kids can ride on a camel and spin around on an antique carousel.

Tidefest Art Fairm, Gig Harbor High School. For the sole purpose of celebrating winter, this event offers arts and crafts, food, and music. Some go just to admire the fine artwork by local artists.

Argosy Christmas Ship Festival, Tacoma. This holiday celebration of more than 6 decades sends flotillas of ships sailing to more than 4 dozen waterfront communities, carrying decks of carolers who perform for the crowds waiting ashore.

Weeklong Model Train Festival, Tacoma. Washington State History Museum organizes this weeklong celebration of the "golden days" of rail travel in the West, with exhibitions of different model trains. Visitors can also check out a permanent model train display.

Other Recommended Restaurants and Lodging . . . .

GIG HARBOR
Brix, 7707 Pioneer Way; (253) 858-6626; www.harborbrix.com. For a fine dining experience, whether the choice is grilled rib eye steak, seared chicken fettuccine, or ravioli Bolognese. Perfect for celebrating special events.

The Maritime Inn, 3212 Harborview Dr.; (253) 858-1818; www.maritimeinn.com. A boutique hotel along the waterfront. Just steps away from restaurants, shops, and galleries.

Waterfront Inn Bed & Breakfast, 9017 N. Harborview Dr.; (253) 857-0770; www.waterfront-inn.com. Seven guest rooms in a beautiful home near the waterfront, which guests can explore with house kayaks. Serves a deluxe continental breakfast of fruit, yogurt, and fresh pastries that can be enjoyed in one's room or on the deck.

TACOMA
Corina Bakery, 510 6th Ave.; (253) 627-5070; www.corinabakery.com. Cozy bakery that turns out quality muffins and special-occasion cakes. Winner of "Tacoma's Best" in scones, bread, and cheesecake. Open daily.

Chinaberry Hill, 302 Tacoma Ave. N; (866) 538-0187; www.chinaberryhill.com. A beautifully furnished 1889 boutique hotel with views of Puget Sound. Easy access to Tacoma sights. Surrounded by lush, well-maintained gardens. Full breakfast.

Green Cape Cod Bed & Breakfast, 2711 N. Warner, (253) 752-1977 or (866) 752-1977; www.greencapecod.com. A short distance from the University of Puget Sound. Three light, airy rooms, all with private baths and views of Commencement Bay. Tacoma-made favorite Almond Roca at each bedside. Visitors praise the salmon quiche and the French toast. Outstanding hospitality.

Hotel Murano, 1320 Broadway Plaza; (888) 862-3255; www.hotelmuranotacoma.com. Trendy hotel centrally located in downtown Tacoma. Classy art collection always on display.

Over the Moon Cafe, 709 Opera Alley; (253) 284-3722; www.overthemooncafe.net. Homemade soups and desserts. Emphasis on Italian and French fare. Steamed clams and wild rice crab cakes are on small plates menu. Bourbon-glazed wild salmon and creamy sage chicken for those wanting a complete dinner. Hard-to-resist desserts. Open for lunch and dinner.

Paddy Coyne's Irish Pub, 815 Pacific Ave.; (253) 272-6963; www.paddycoynes.net. Located in the historic Hotel Olympus building with a bar said to have come all the way from France, and hand-crafted by Franciscan monks in 1897. Traditional Irish food, including bangers and mash, shepherd's pie, and Irish soda bread.

For More Information . . . .

Gig Harbor/Peninsula Chamber of Commerce, 3311 Harborview Dr., Suite 101, Gig Harbor, WA 98332; (253) 851-6865; www.gigharborchamber.com.

Tacoma–Pierce County Chamber of Commerce, 950 Pacific Ave., Suite 300, Tacoma, WA 98402; (253) 627-2175; www.tacoma chamber.org.

Tacoma Visitor Information Center, 1516 Pacific Ave., Tacoma, WA 98402; (253) 627-2836 or (800) 272-2662; www.travel tacoma.com.

Tacoma Link Light Rail, Sound Transit, 401 S. Jackson St., Seattle, WA 98104; (206) 398-5000 or (800) 201-4900; www.soundtransit .org. One of the best ways to get around downtown Tacoma. Links with the Dome station, a regional hub for commuter transportation.

WESTBOUND ESCAPE *Two*
Poulsbo to Port Townsend
INVESTIGATING PUGET SOUND'S ARCHITECTURAL
TREASURES / 1 NIGHT

- Award-winning historic downtown
- Boutique shopping
- Fort Worden State Park
- Kayaking
- Norwegian settlement
- Marine science centers

This excursion begins in the Scandinavian town of **Poulsbo,** on Liberty Bay, a slice of waterfront heaven that reminded the early Scandinavian settlers of the fjords in their home country. Fishers, loggers, and farmers, mainly from Norway in the late 1880s, were the first to settle in the region. The community still takes pride in its roots, carefully maintaining a charming Scandinavian facade on its Front Street storefronts. **Port Gamble,** another historic village on the National Register of Historic Places, sits on the northern-most tip of Kitsap Peninsula. Founded by New Englanders, primarily from Maine, in the mid-19th century, the architectural styles clearly reflect their roots. The towering elms lining Main Street were brought around Cape Horn from Maine in 1872. Much of Port Townsend, which is divided between a downtown waterfront district and a residential area on a bluff above it, is a designated National Historic District. Victorian homes and commercial buildings, built in the late 19th century when Port Townsend was expected to become a great seaport, have been restored with pride.

The fact that all three communities pay homage to earlier pioneer roots, makes this 1-night escape a delicious multicultural adventure.

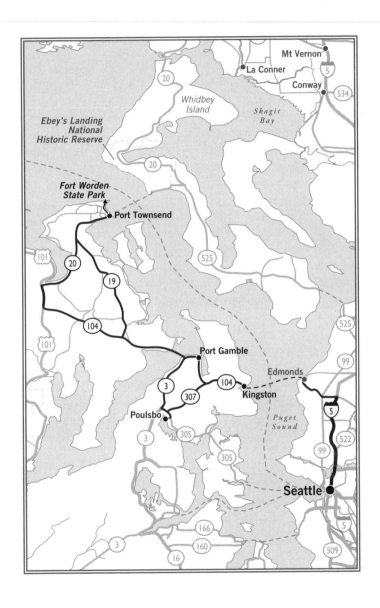

DAY 1 / MORNING

From Seattle, follow I-5 north and then exit on SR 104 to the Edmonds/Kingston Ferry Terminal. Take the ferry to **Kingston,** a former lumber town that's now called the "Little City by the Sea." Travel southwest on SR 104 to SR 307, then drive on SR 305 southeast to Lincoln Road, which winds down to Front Street and Poulsbo's waterfront. You will know you have arrived at this Little Norway on the Fjord when you read the welcoming mural: VELKOMMEN TIL POULSBO, which you can translate as "Welcome to Paul's place."

The inhabitants of Poulsbo closely identify with the marine life, as witnessed by the three marinas on their small waterfront. Take time to also walk along the exquisitely scenic 600-foot boardwalk at **Waterfront Park** overlooking Liberty Bay and Puget Sound. Stroll **Liberty Bay Park,** which is connected by a wooden causeway over the water to **American Legion Park,** to soak up more maritime flavor. Pennants snap in the wind on fishing and pleasure boats as they come and go in the busy harbor. Liberty Bay has a picnic area and a covered pavilion that is used during the summer for dancing, concerts, and arts festivals.

Front Street is lined with picturesque Norwegian-style restaurants, galleries, and shops. Every shutter and door is adorned with the decorative folk art, rosemaling, often characterized by stylized flower ornamentation and scrollwork. But before you continue your stroll, have some lunch.

LUNCH **Tizley's Europub,** 18928 Front St.; (360) 394-0080. Schnitzel sandwiches, garlic rosemary chicken sandwiches, and classic Reubens are among the many selections here. Specials might include a sausage plate or a Scandinavian platter.

AFTERNOON

Visit **Verksted Gallery,** 18937 Front St. NE (360-697-4470), an artist co-op stocked with wood carvings, leather work, hand-painted shirts, chocolate sculpture, and cribbage boards made from elk horn.

Browse the shops along Front Street for unusual souvenirs, such as the brass and nautical items in **Cargo Hold** (www.cargohold .com); the **Nordic Maid,** for authentic Scandinavian books, dala horses, and candleholders (www.nordicmaid.com); and elegant custom designed jewelry at **Blue Heron Jewelry** (www.blueheron jewelry.com). The fragrance will draw you to **Sluy's Bakery,** 18924 Front St NE (360-697-2253), where fresh-baked breads and pastries vie for attention. Specialties are the Doughboy, a big gingerbread man–shaped doughnut, and the Viking Cup, a cinnamon roll with cream cheese icing.

At the **Poulsbo Marine Science Center,** 18743 Front St. NE (360-779-5549), on Liberty Bay, you can examine sea life under microscopes, touch anemones, see ghost shrimp, and watch videos and documentaries.

Leaving Poulsbo, take SR 3 north to **Port Gamble** on the shores of the scenic Hood Canal. You will develop a keener appreciation for this town by following the Walking Tour of Historic Port Gamble (www.portgamble.com/pdf/port_gamble_walking_tour.pdf). Port Gamble was once a company town for employees of Pope & Talbot, a lumber and shipping firm. Although P&T closed its mill in 1995, the company nevertheless made a commitment to rebuild and restore dozens of buildings that represent a range of architectural styles, many of which are on the walking tour. The oldest house is the Thompson house, built in 1859; the newest is an automotive repair and gas station built in the 1920s, a building said to symbolize a rise in automobile purchases, which reduced the need for the compact company town concept. Visit **Port Gamble Museum,** 1 View Dr. (360-297-8074). Furniture settings are the backdrop to the interesting story of one of the last company towns in the Pacific Northwest. If you haven't had breakfast, stop by the Tea Room at Port Gamble, 32279 Rainier St., for their elegant "Breakfast Tea" of quiche, fruit tart, scones and jam, and fruit cup; less elaborate fare includes soups and salads. The shop also carries an enormous variety of black, green, and white teas, and hand-crafted chocolate truffles and fudge.

To get to **Port Townsend,** drive on SR 104 west to SR 20.

Through the trees you'll catch glimpses of pleasure boats on Admiralty Inlet as you continue north to Port Townsend. The town was named in 1792 by Captain George Vancouver in honor of an English marquis, although the town wasn't officially established until 1851, when the first settlers built a log cabin at the corner of Water and Tyler Streets. The community grew, and its prospects as a center of commerce seemed limitless until the transcontinental railroad was laid—and stopped at Seattle.

Out on the peninsula, Port Townsend was left to languish until its charm as a little-changed Victorian seaport was recognized in the 1970s. Now it booms with tourism and as an arts center where artists from around the state display and sell their wares.

At the chamber of commerce office, pick up brochures and a tour map that describes 72 historic homes and sites. Continue into town to the end of Water Street and the city hall, newly renovated to accommodate the **Jefferson County Historical Society Museum,** 540 Water St. (360-385-1003; www.jchsmuseum.org). Well-conceived and well-preserved exhibits on the region's Native Americans and early Chinese inhabitants, the Victorian era, and military and maritime memorabilia make a stop here worthwhile. Open Fri through Mon, 11 a.m. to 4 p.m. Park your car in this area; most of the tour is easy walking from here.

DINNER **The Fountain Cafe,** 920 Washington St.; (360) 385-1364. Small, unpretentious restaurant on a hillside above downtown. Sublime chowder, pastas, dinners, and desserts. Sooner or later everyone stops for ice cream or a delectable espresso-chip brownie at **Elevated Ice Cream;** 627 Water St.; (360) 385-1156; www.elevatedicecream.com. The bright little shop is reputed to have the best ice cream in the state.

LODGING **The Inn at McCurdy House,** 405 Taylor St.; (360) 379-4824; www.innatmccurdyhouse.com. Lovingly restored older home with 2 suites. Close to the historic center, but situated on a bluff, so ambience is quiet and restful. Full breakfast served in the dining room or on the deck, with views of beautifully landscaped gardens.

DAY 2 / MORNING

BREAKFAST Enjoy a well-rounded breakfast at the **Inn at McCurdy House.**

As you stroll along Port Townsend's tree-lined streets, notice **Haller Fountain,** Taylor and Washington Streets. The bronze figure, variously named Galatea, Venus, and Innocence, was shown at the Chicago Exhibition of 1893. It was donated to Port Townsend by Theodore Haller in honor of the early pioneers. The spreading **Chinese Tree of Heaven,** now more than 150 years old, is said to be a gift from the emperor of China. It was intended for San Francisco, but the ship carrying it was blown off course near Port Townsend. As thanks for his happy stay here, the ship's captain left the tree. **Jefferson County Courthouse,** on Jefferson Street, was built in 1892. The castlelike building is one of the two oldest courthouses still in use in the state, and its 100-foot clock tower is a beacon to sailors. The **Old Bell Tower** on a bluff at Tyler and Jefferson Streets, overlooking the downtown district, dates from 1890. It's the only one of its kind in the United States. The 1868 **Rothschild House State Park,** Taylor and Franklin Streets (360-385-1003), is the home of an early Port Townsend merchant. Now a state park, the home is listed on both State and National Registers of Historic Places. It is open for tours daily in summer, weekends in winter.

Ann Starrett Mansion, 744 Clay St. (360-385-3205 or 800-321-0644; www.starrettmansion.com), the most elaborate Victorian mansion in Port Townsend, was built in 1899 in classic stick style. Its circular staircase, ceiling frescoes, and elaborate furnishings make afternoon tours popular with visitors. The house is now in use as a bed-and-breakfast inn.

After your walking tour of this waterfront town, check the myriad shops on Water Street and "Uptown," a business district on Lawrence Street that was originally begun so that respectable ladies would not have to venture to the rougher waterfront area to shop.

LUNCH   **Silverwater Cafe,** 237 Taylor St.; (360) 385-6448; www .silverwatercafe.com. Closed Sun. Clam chowder is served every day, and 2 other soups rotate daily. Many other choices to satisfy, too: Washington apple salad, and a special take on the BLT, called b.l.t.r.t.c., with roast turkey and cream cheese on a baguette; several meat and meatless burger varieties, and other items, too.

After lunch, a drive out to **Fort Worden State Park,** 200 Battery Way (360-344-4400; www.parks.wa.gov/fortworden), will take you to the filming location of *An Officer and a Gentleman*. Built at the turn of the 20th century as a base to defend Puget Sound, Fort Worden is a 330-acre estate with an army cemetery, officers' quarters, a theater, parade grounds, gun emplacements, bronze foundry, and Point Wilson Light Station.

At the **Port Townsend Marine Science Center,** Fort Worden State Park, 532 Battery Way (360-385-5582; www.ptmsc.org), in a historic building on the public fishing pier at Fort Worden, visitors can touch and handle sea creatures at open "wet tables." Starfish, sea cucumbers, tubeworms, and other marine life live in the touch tanks. The center holds classes in marine ecology, shows informative slide shows, and runs workshops. It's open afternoons in summer, Tuesday through Sunday, and weekends in fall and spring.

Stop at **Chetzemoka Park** to stroll the grassy grounds and enjoy the fragrant rose garden. The park, named for a Clallam Indian chief, has a bandstand, picnic tables, playground equipment, and access to the beach. Now that you are completely rejuvenated, take the drive home, beginning on SR 20, then turning south on SR 19 and east on SR 104 to Kingston, where you will take the ferry.

There's More . . . .

PORT GAMBLE
Farms. **Sawdust Hill Alpaca Farm,** 25448 Port Gamble Rd. NE; (360) 286-9999; www.sawdusthillalpacas.com. Working farm 4 miles north of Poulsbo. Fiber artists will find particular joy in browsing the gift shop, and buying alpaca yarn and raw fiber. Tours daily from 11 a.m. to 2 p.m.

Museums. **Of Sea and Shore Museum,** 1 Rainier Ave.; (360) 297-2426; www.ofseaandshore.com/main.php. In the historic General Store Building, open daily 9 a.m. to 5 p.m. Free admission. Museum collection is one of the largest private shell collections in the United States.

PORT TOWNSEND
Art galleries. **First Saturday Gallery Walk**. On the first Sat evening of the month, galleries and studios are open late.

Bicycling. The city of Port Townsend lends bicycles; find them at various downtown locations, such as the corner of Quincy and Water Streets.

Kayaking. Port Townsend Outdoors, 1017-B Water St.; (360) 379-3608 or (888) 754-8598; www.ptoutdoors.com. Offers guided kayak tours for the whole family, kayak rentals, and individual lessons.

POULSBO

Kayaking. Kayak rentals at **Olympic Outdoor Center,** 18971 Front St; (360) 697-6095. Near the aquarium. Paddle around Liberty Bay.

Parks. Raab Park, at Caldart Avenue off Hostmark Street. Poulsbo's largest park. Fourteen acres of grassy slopes provide covered picnic facilities, barbecue grills, a playground, horseshoe pits, a sand volleyball court, and an outdoor stage.

Special Events . . . .

MID-MAY
Rhododendron Festival, Port Townsend. Parade, bed race, flower show, arts and crafts fair, dancing, and fireworks.

Viking Fest, Poulsbo. A celebration of Norwegian heritage, with Scandinavian fare and native dancing. There's also a Viking road race and a Miss Viking Fest Pageant.

LATE JULY
Port Townsend Jazz Festival. Musicians from around the country perform on the Fort Worden main stage and in the downtown pubs.

LATE SEPTEMBER

Historic Homes Tours, Port Townsend. Self-guided tours of the city's Victorian architecture, from mansions and cottages to country inns and public buildings.

Other Recommended Restaurants and Lodging . . . .

PORT TOWNSEND

Ann Starrett Mansion, 744 Clay St.; (360) 385-3205 or (800) 321-0644; www.starrettmansion.com. Most opulent bed-and-breakfast in town. Historic home embellished with Victorian gingerbread. Eleven guest rooms. Full breakfast.

Blue Gull Inn Bed & Breakfast, 1310 Clay St.; (360) 379-3241 or (888) 700-0205; www.bluegullinn.com. An 1868 Victorian with a large, welcoming porch. Six pastel-hued rooms with private baths. Large breakfasts may include blueberry crepes, pecan praline French toast, or savory green chili quiche.

Bread and Roses Bakery, 230 Quincy St.; (360) 385-1044. Home-baked pastries, soups, sandwiches, espresso.

Fort Worden State Park, 200 Battery Way; park (360) 344-4434; hostel (360) 385-0655. From campsites and hostel dorm wards to rooms in Officers' Row with Victorian decor and modern comforts, Fort Worden has options for everyone. Two campgrounds, one in a forested area and the other at Point Wilson beach. Both have rest-rooms and showers. Make your reservation early.

Ravenscroft Inn, 533 Quincy St.; (360) 385-2784 or (800) 782-2691; www.ravenscroftinn.com. Eight spacious rooms in a hillside colonial-style inn. Peaceful atmosphere, full breakfast.

Salal Cafe, 634 Water St.; (360) 385-6532. Healthy home-style foods; vegetarian entrees available. Plant-filled solarium. Voted region's "Best Breakfast" for the past 4 years.

POULSBO

The Bayside Broiler, 18779 Front St.; (360) 779-9076. Waterfront restaurant offering seafood, soups, salads, steaks, and chops, along with views of the Olympic Mountains.

For More Information . . . .

Jefferson County Chamber Visitor Center, 440 12th St., Port Townsend, WA 98368; (360) 385-2722; www.enjoypt.com or www .ptchamber.org.

Kitsap Peninsula Visitor and Convention Bureau, 9481 Silverdale Way NW, Suite 281, Silverdale, WA 98383; (800) 337-0580; www .visitkitsap.com.

Poulsbo Chamber of Commerce, 19351 8th Ave NE, #108, Poulsbo, WA 98370-8710; (360) 779-4848; www.poulsbochamber.com.

WESTBOUND ESCAPE *Three*
Sequim to Port Angeles to Victoria
SATURATING THE SENSES: FROM LAVENDER FIELDS
TO HIGH TEA / 1 NIGHT

This escape takes you from the drier climate in the Sequim-Dungeness Valley to the coastal climates in Port Angeles and Victoria, British Columbia. In Sequim, everything's tinted lavender. It's no wonder, with the more than 110,000 lavender plants growing each year in the Sequim-Dungeness Valley. If you take this trip in mid-July, you can attend the Sequim Lavender Festival in the morning and immerse yourself in heavenly scents, before driving to Port Angeles for a stroll and lunch. In Port Angeles, you will board the ferry to Victoria for an overnight stay. Just 90 minutes away by boat, Victoria will wow you with its distinctly different culture.

> Butchart Gardens
> Castles
> Outdoor sculptures
> Lavender farms
> Historical museums
> Royal B.C. Museum

DAY 1 / MORNING

Follow I-5 north. Exit on SR 104 to the Edmonds/Kingston Ferry Terminal. Take the ferry to Kingston, then drive north on SR 3 to Port Gamble and northwest on SR 104.

Sequim is justifiably proud of its title as the **Lavender Capital of North America.** But the city's residents haven't always felt this way. In 1995 residents of the Sequim Prairie were worried about losing the longtime agricultural base to commercial and residential development. Knowing that Sequim was well suited for lavender

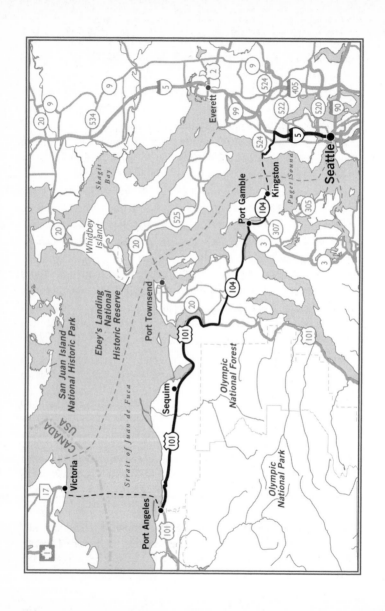

crops, a group of community activists decided to restore the rich agricultural history. They promoted lavender crops as a way to revive the region's economic base.

Try to plan this escape in mid-July, during the annual **Sequim Lavender Festival** (www.lavenderfestival.com), when you can tour lavender farms, browse a large street fair showcasing the work of more than 150 vendors from across the United States, listen to music, and sip lavender tea. Notice that lavender is used in count-less ways, from fragrance and medicine to decor and food.

However, Sequim is a wonderful place to visit anytime. Many of the lavender farms are open year-round. Just a sampling are **Cedarbrook Lavender & Herb Farm** (www.cedarbrooklavender.com), **Jardin du Soleil Lavender** (www.jardindusoleil.com), **Lost Mountain Lavender** (www.lostmountainlavender.com), **Olympic Lavender Farm** (www.olympiclavender.com), **Purple Haze Lavender Farm** (www.purplehazelavender.com), and **Sunshine Herb and Lavender Farm** (www.sunshinelavender.com).

LUNCH   **Alder Wood Bistro,** 139 West Alder St.; (360) 683-4321; www.alderwoodbistro.com. Pesto chicken or wood-fired vegetable pizzas, warm campfire chicken or portobello paninis, sweet potato fries, and other fine morsels at this casual neighborhood restaurant.

DAY 1 / AFTERNOON

After lunch in Sequim, drive 17 miles west to **Port Angeles,** which becomes US 101. On your right is the **Strait of Juan de Fuca,** a wide channel that defines the border between Washington and Van-couver Island, British Columbia. On your left, the Olympic Range rises 7,000 feet, snow-clad and craggy.

If it's a weekday, tour the **Clallam County Historical Museum,** 223 E. 4th St. (360-417-2364; open 10 a.m. to 4 p.m. Mon through Fri). Located on the second floor of the 2-story Georgian-style brick building that once served as the county courthouse, the museum features exhibits of early maritime activities and the development of First Nations languages, offering a glimpse into days well before the area was settled. The first floor of the building serves as the headquarters for the Clallam County Historical Society, which maintains large collections of old photographs, maps, and documents.

The courthouse itself is intriguing. Built in 1914 and now on the state and national historic registers, it has a stained-glass skylight, a clock tower, and a view of Port Angeles harbor 4 blocks down the hill.

Admire 4 dozen pieces of public art, mainly metal sculpture, between W. 1st Street and Front Street. View the city's brochure at www.portangelesdowntown.com/files/Brochure062409c%20Final %20SCREEN.pdf. On a clear day you can see across the strait to downtown Victoria.

Begin your visit to **Victoria** by driving, or walking, onto a ferry, and experience that British Columbian city for yourself. The ferry takes you to Victoria's Inner Harbor, a good place to take a stroll and people watch, and the nearby Causeway, where performers entertain passers-by. Remember that US citizens returning from Canada by land or sea are required to present a US passport.

DINNER **Aura Waterfront Restaurant & Patio,** 680 Montreal St.; (250) 386-8721; www.aurarestaurant.ca. Seafood, vegetarian ravioli, and beef are some of the dinner entrees. If you want an earlier but equally fine menu, the restaurant lounge serves delicious lighter fare. Seasonal, local organic produce and ocean-friendly seafood options are the winners here.

LODGING **Albion Manor Bed & Breakfast,** 224 Superior St.; (877) 389-0012; www.albionmanor.com. The 1892 home is a registered historical landmark, within a 5-minute walk to downtown Victoria and the ferry terminal. Fine Victorian-style furnishings add charm to your accommodations, while modern bathroom fixtures and in some cases Jacuzzis provide the ultimate in comfort.

DAY 2 / MORNING

BREAKFAST   **Albion Manor Bed & Breakfast.** Soufflé pancakes and Milanese frittata are among the rotating gourmet delights at this B&B.

Victoria is the capital city of the province of British Columbia. The **Parliament Buildings,** reflecting the Romanesque revival architecture, are right on the inner harbor, on Belleville Street. The buildings were constructed in 1893. During the summer, visitor tours run daily. This is a fine opportunity to see the legislative process and learn about British Columbia's political history.

You won't be able to see everything during your short visit to the **Royal B.C. Museum,** 675 Belleville St. (250-356-7226 or 888-447-7977; www.royalbcmuseum.bc.ca). One satisfying way to appreciate this remarkable museum of human and natural history is to select 1 or 2 exhibits, such as the First Nations Gallery, where you will enter the house of Chief Kwakwabalasami, or the Modern History Gallery, with a replica of the stern section of Captain George Vancouver's ship HMS *Discovery,* and a diorama of the Tremblay family homestead. The natural history exhibit pays particular attention to the ways the environment shapes the province's landscape. Perhaps you would rather take time in the National Geographic IMAX theater on site, with showings that range from featuring the Hubble space telescope to Vincent Van Gogh's short but profound history.

The **Emily Carr House,** 207 Government St. (250-383-5843; www.emilycarr.com), may be your only opportunity to learn about Canada's most renowned artist and see 18 of her original works.

She painted the western B.C. landscape and Native villages with the eye of an anthropologist. Carr was born in this house, and numerous family artifacts are displayed in her bedroom.

The building that houses the **Maritime Museum,** 28 Bastion Square (250-385-4222; www.mmbc.bc.ca), once was British Columbia's Supreme Court. Take a few moments to visit the 19th-century courtroom upstairs. Naturally, the predominant exhibits focus on shipbuilding, shipwrecks, and water-faring vessels—from canoes to coastal steamships and B.C. ferries.

Before you leave Victoria by ferry, stop by **Side Street Studio,** 737 Humboldt St. (250-590-4644; www.sidestreetstudio.com). It's the place to buy hand-crafted items made by B.C. artists: greeting cards, pottery, glasswork, jewelry, and truly one-of-a-kind West Coast art.

There's More . . . .

PORT ANGELES

Aquarium. **Feiro Marine Life Center,** City Pier at the foot of Lincoln and Railroad Streets; (360) 417-6254; www.feiromarinelifecenter .org. Displays of local marine specimens, including a large octopus. Starfish and other creatures in the touch tank.

Art galleries. **Port Angeles Fine Art Center,** 1203 E. Lauridsen Blvd.; (360) 417-4590. An award-winning home on 5 parklike acres overlooking the city, with views of the mountains and water. Visual arts exhibitions are shown year-round.

Fishing. **Port Angeles Charters,** 1014 Marine Dr.; (360) 457-7629. Represents 3 charter fishing companies in the area. Salmon season starts in late spring, closes Sept. Bottom fishing from Feb to Nov.

Parks. **City Pier.** This shoreline park has an observation tower, lawns, picnic area, boat moorage, and promenade decks.

SEQUIM

Golf. **Dungeness Golf Course,** 1965 Woodcock Rd.; (800) 447-6826. Eighteen-hole course, driving range, clubhouse, restaurant.

Wildlife. **Dungeness Spit.** Longest sand jetty in the United States, 7 miles of sand, agates, and driftwood. National Wildlife Refuge with waterfowl, shorebirds, seals.

Zoos. **Olympic Game Farm,** 1423 Ward Rd.; (360) 683-4295 or (800) 778-4295; www.olygamefarm.com. For 40 years, home to endangered animals, such as timber wolves and Bengal tigers and the more common but fascinating coyote and bobcats.

VICTORIA

Gardens. **Butchart Gardens,** 800 Benvenuto Ave., Brentwood Bay; (250) 652-5256; www.butchartgardens.com. Fourteen miles north of Victoria, open every day at 9 a.m. except for Christmas Day, when it opens at 1 p.m. Once an abandoned pit, Butchart is world renowned for its magnificent showcase garden. Afternoon tea is served year-round.

Neighborhoods. **Chinatown,** 500–600 block of Fisgard St. Canada's oldest Chinatown is characterized by narrow, winding streets and lots of little shops and restaurants.

Historic Sites. **Craigdarroch Castle,** 1050 Joan Crescent; (250) 592-5323; www.thecastle.ca. Open daily. Craigdarroch was built between 1887 and 1890 for Robert Dunsmuir, a Scottish immigrant who made his fortune from Vancouver Island coal. This legendary Victorian mansion, with 4 floors of exquisite stained-glass windows, intricate woodwork, and fabulous Victorian-era furnishings, is built on a hill overlooking the City of Victoria. (Craigdarroch means "rocky, oak place" in Gaelic.)

Hatley Park and Hatley Castle, 2005 Sooke Rd.; (866) 241-0674 or (250) 391-2666; www.hatleycastle.com. Twenty-five minutes from downtown Victoria. One of Canada's largest and most diverse National Historic Sites, the park has hundreds of Heritage Trees. Hatley Castle Museum houses artifacts and exhibits from the days when the property was a Coastal Salish Indian burial site, to the present time as campus of Royal Roads University.

Helmcken House, 675 Belleville St.; (250) 356-7226; www .royalbcmuseum.bc.ca/RBCM_Cult_Pre/Helmcken_Hse.aspx. Dr. John Sebastian Helmcken was a surgeon with the Hudson's Bay Company. This is one of the oldest houses in British Columbia on its original premises.

St. Ann's Academy, 835 Humbolt St.; (250) 953-8828; www .stannsacademy.com. May be the oldest building in Victoria, built by Jacques Lequechier in 1844. Has been a rectory and schoolhouse, then a convent and school for the sisters of St. Ann. The nuns gave the school to the museum in 1974 when it was moved to its present location behind Helmcken House on Elliott Square. Free.

Theater. **Royal Theater,** 805 Broughton St.; (250) 386-6121; www .rmts.bc.ca/royaltheatre/index.aspx. The 1,434-seat Royal Theatre, opened in 1913 as the Victoria Opera House, is home of the Victoria Symphony, Pacific Opera Victoria, and other locally produced entertainment.

Special Events . . . .

APRIL-OCTOBER
Sequim Open Air Market. For 15 years has been selling fresh produce, plants, and flowers. Locally crafted jewelry, soaps, clothing, and pottery, a wide range of foods, and community-service booths.

MAY
Irrigation Festival, Sequim. Oldest festival in Washington; features parade, fireworks, logging show.

AUGUST
Clallam County Fair, Port Angeles. Carnival, entertainment, cribbage tournament, agriculture barn, and model train demonstrations.

EARLY SEPTEMBER
Port Angeles Strait Bluegrass Festival. Features top bands from the Pacific Northwest and Canada.

SEPTEMBER
Glass Art Festival, Sequim. Glass art show. Glass Alley, where glass artists sell their wares. Glass art on display in businesses and shops across town.

Other Recommended Restaurants and Lodging . . . .

PORT ANGELES
A Hidden Haven & Water Garden Cottages, 1428 Dan Kelley Rd.; (360) 452-2719 or (877) 418-0938. Gorgeous cottages tucked away on 20 acres of ultraprivate property that includes multiple gardens, waterfalls, and ponds. One room, 2 suites, and 5 cottages, all romantic and all elegantly decorated.

Bella Italia, 118 E. 1st. St.; (360) 457-5442; www.bellaitaliapa .com. Offers a menu that pleases both kids and discerning adults. You can fill up on assorted antipasti plates or large salads, pasta dishes, and meat or seafood entrees.

Cafe Garden, 1506 E. 1st St.; (360) 457-4611; www.cafegarden pa.com. Open for breakfast, lunch, and dinner. Seafood and pasta salads. Sandwiches, pastas, crab cakes, and quesadillas, all cooked to perfection.

Chestnut Cottage, 929 E. Front St.; (360) 452-8344. The breakfast menu touts luscious eggs Benedict and strawberry blintzes, and laudable salads and fresh pastas for lunch. The atmosphere is stylish but not overdone. Owner Diane Nagler also owns **First Street Haven** (360-457-0352), a delightful little place at 107 1st St. that serves huge omelets, large portions of eggs, and perfectly prepared hash browns. At lunch, fresh-baked breads and large wraps are made on the spot.

Colette's Bed & Breakfast, 339 Finn Hall Rd.; (360) 457-9197. An oceanside estate on 10 acres. All 5 suites have ocean views and private patios for the perfect romantic getaway. Each has access to a sanctuary of gardens and forests. Frittatas, crepes, fresh fruit, and fresh-baked pastries are among the carefully prepared breakfast dishes.

Downtown Hotel, 101½ E. Front St.; (360) 565-1125 or (866) 688-8600; www.portangelesdowntownhotel.com. Offers a terrific price for its European-style rooms with bathrooms and showers just down the hall. Rooms and suites with private baths also available.

Tudor Inn, 1108 S. Oak; (360) 452-3138 or (866) 286-2224. Voted "2006 Best Bed-and-Breakfast in Clallam County." Five guest rooms, all with private baths and views of the Olympic Mountains or the Strait of Juan de Fuca. Gourmet breakfasts and late-night snacks. Innkeeper packs a sack breakfast for visitors taking the early-morning ferry to Victoria.

Wildfire Grill, 929 W. 8th St.; (360) 452-0400; http://wildfire grillpa.homestead.com. A bit off the beaten path, but well worth the stop, say frequent visitors who appreciate the warm and inviting atmosphere, and more important, the homemade salad dressings, entrees of carefully prepared beef short ribs, blackened steelhead salmon, and glazed pork loin with fig reduction, along with sides of ultra-fluffy mashed potatoes and fresh flatbread. Nice outdoor seating area.

SEQUIM

Bell St. Bakery, 173 West Bell St.; (360) 681-6262; www.bell streetbakery.com. Organic in-house milled artisan breads, including their own locally developed Sequim sourdough artisan bread, make a great addition to a picnic basket. They also serve lunch in this homelike retail store: soups, sandwiches, and homemade pizzas, as well as cinnamon rolls, scones, and fresh croissants for midmorning snacks.

Bond Ranch Retreat, 1405 Hooker Rd.; (360) 461-2156; www .bondranchretreat.com. Four guest rooms and a cottage, tidy and cozy, with just a few frills. Breakfast baskets delivered to all guest rooms. On a luscious piece of property, with a covered patio for savoring fresh country air and a morning cup of coffee.

Dockside Grill, 2577 W. Sequim Bay Rd.; (360) 683-7510 or (888) 640-7226; www.docksidegrill-sequim.com. Sandwiches and salads for lunch. Pastas with and without seafood, plus cedar-plank salmon or steak, coconut-crusted prawns, and paella. All come with views of the Olympic Peninsula. This a place to celebrate that special occasion.

Groveland Cottage Bed and Breakfast, 4861 Sequim-Dungeness Way; (360) 683-3565 or (800) 879-8859; www.grovelandcottage .com. Four individually decorated rooms with private baths, built in 1886. One "secret" cottage nestled in lovely gardens. The bed-and-breakfast also organizes crab-walk tours, bicycling tours, and golf packages.

Lost Mountain Lodge, 303 Sunny View Dr.; (888) 683-2431 or (360) 683-2431; www.lostmountainlodge.com. Rated in "Best Places to Kiss on the Olympic Peninsula," with 4 spacious fireplace suites and a large vacation cottage on 9 acres that are designated a National Wildlife Federation Certified Wildlife Habitat. Full breakfast included in rates.

Sunshine Cafe, 145 W. Washington St.; (360) 682-4282. Great for families. Quality standard egg breakfasts, old-fashioned oatmeal and Cream of Wheat, corned beef hash, and personally designed pancakes with real maple syrup. Salads and homemade soups are popular at lunch, and so are the fresh-baked pies.

VICTORIA
Abbeymoore Manor Bed and Breakfast Inn, 1470 Rockland Ave.; (250) 370-1470 or (888) 801-1811; www.abbeymoore.com. This lodging is a very good price, considering the spaciousness, the furnishings, and the amenities. Multi-course gourmet breakfast, such as blueberry stuffed French toast and Thai prawn omelets.

Abigail's Hotel, 906 McClure St.; (800) 561-6565; www.abigails hotel.com. Calls itself a boutique bed-and-breakfast hotel. The rooms are spacious and exquisitely furnished. Gourmet breakfast and welcome basket with cookies. Hors d'oeuvres served at 5 p.m. A special place for a special occasion.

Cafe Brio, 944 Fort St.; (250) 383-0009; www.cafe-brio.com. Serves truly original fare, using a variety of Italian cured meats. Prepares several seafood dishes, and luscious desserts. *Northwest Palate* magazine has praised the cafe's use of local, organic ingredients. Open every night for dinner.

Red Fish Blue Fish, 1006 Wharf St.; (250) 298-6877; www.red fish-bluefish.com. Wild Pacific salmon, halibut, or cod, with chips, of course. Cone-shaped tortillas stuffed with fish and condiments.

Restaurant Matisse, 512 Yates St.; (250) 480-0883; www.restaurant matisse.com. Lovingly prepared French classics: duck, venison, and lamb entrees, and fine desserts, in an elegant atmosphere.

Wild Saffron Bistro, 1605 Store St.; (250) 361-3150; www.swans hotel.com/bistro.php. Located in the Wild Swan Hotel. Voted among the top 10 restaurants in Victoria. Salmon pasta, smoked tofu, and pan-roasted fresh duck represent entrees on this innovative menu.

Wild Swan Hotel, 1605 Store St.; (250) 361-3150; www.swans hotel.com/hotel/index.php. Located in historic Victoria. A variety of chic suites suitable for families. It exhibits an enormous art collection, some of which is for sale.

For More Information . . . .

B.C. Ferries, 1112 Fort St., Victoria, BC V8V 4V2; (888) BC FERRY (888-223-3779); www.bcferries.com.

Black Ball Ferry Line, 101 E. Railroad Ave., Port Angeles, WA 98362; (360) 457-4491; www.cohoferry.com. Between Port Angeles and Victoria.

British Columbia Tourism, P.O. Box 9830, Police Station and Provincial Government Headquarters, Victoria, BC V8T 5C3; (800) 435-5622; www.hellobc.com. Official travel planning site of Tourism, British Columbia.

North Olympic Peninsula Visitor & Convention Bureau, 338 W. 1st St., No. 104, P.O. Box 670, Port Angeles, WA 98362; (360) 452-8552; www.olympicpeninsula.org.

Port Angeles Chamber of Commerce, 121 E. Railroad Ave., Port Angeles, WA 98362; (360) 452-2363 or (877) 456-8372; www.portangeles.org.

Royal Tours, (888) 381-1800; www.royaltours.ca. Operates daily bus tours to Victoria and Butchart Gardens from Sequim and Port Angeles. Costs include guaranteed ferry boarding and Butchart Gardens admission.

Sequim-Dungeness Valley Chamber of Commerce Visitor Information Center, 1192 E. Washington St., Sequim, WA 98382; (360) 683-6197; www.visitsun.com.

Washington State Ferries, 2901 3rd Ave., Suite 500, Seattle, WA 98121-3014; (206) 464-6400 or (888) 808-7977; www.wsdot.wa.gov/ferries. The ferries all depart from Pier 52.

WESTBOUND ESCAPE *Four*
Olympic Peninsula by Way of Juan de Fuca Strait
EXAMINING FIRST NATIONS HISTORY AND
DENSE RAIN FORESTS / 1 NIGHT

On this escape, your ultimate destination is the Olympic Peninsula in western Washington, a terrain that is intensely green even to visitors from the Pacific Northwest, where much of the landscape is green year-round. Yearly, the Olympic Peninsula and adjacent Hoh Rain Forest receive 140 to

Isolated beaches
Historic lodging
Makah Nations Museum
Rain forests
Timber museum
Wilderness trails

167 inches of rain. The Hoh is one of a few temperate rain forests in the United States, and one of three such forests in the world; the others are in southern Chile and on the west coast of New Zealand. The fragrant evergreen leaves, lacy ferns, and tangled moss are always moist, creating an utterly refreshing sojourn for all who enter. During the summer and fall, when the sun filters through and casts light on the forest floor, the look is almost surreal.

DAY 1 / MORNING

But first, take SR 104 to Edmonds. Take the Edmonds/Kingston ferry to Kingston. Disembark and continue straight on SR 104, merging onto US 101 north toward **Salt Creek Recreation Area.** To your right are stunning views of the Strait of San Juan de Fuca and Vancouver Island, British Columbia.

Turn right at SR 112. After 5.2 miles, you will turn right at Camp Hayden Road, to the 196-acre **Salt Creek County Park**

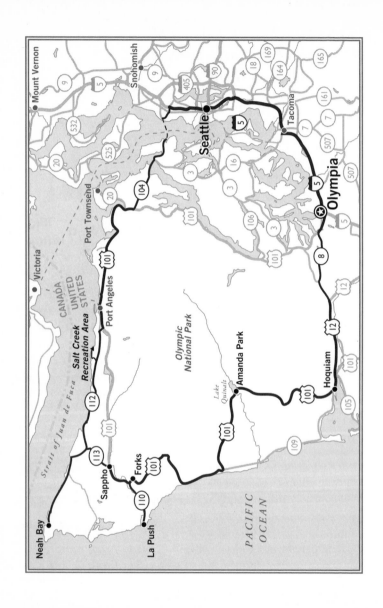

and Campgrounds (www.clallam.net/countyparks). Here, along beaches and hiking trails, you can explore the old Camp Hayden at Striped Peak headland, overlooking the Strait of Juan de Fuca. Your self-guided tour on the site will take you to a formidable gun emplacement built into the hillside. Samples of old artillery shells demonstrate the size of the now-removed guns. One hundred fifty soldiers were stationed here during World War II, manning guns capable of firing a 1-ton projectile 28 miles—reaching across the strait. The adjacent park gives access to **Tongue Point Marine Sanctuary,** where the beaches are rich in tide pools full of sea stars and urchins, barnacles, and anemones. The historic **Joyce General Store** is worth a stop, because it has changed so little in more than 100 years. In the store's jam-packed space, travelers can buy just about anything, from socks, batteries, and cast-iron frying pans to jerky, books, and Chinese soap. Next door, the **Joyce Depot Museum** (www.joycewa.com/museum.htm), a log cabin built of Alaska yellow cedar, displays a classroom and a kitchen setting, railroad memorabilia, and interesting old photos.

Continue on through **Pysht,** once a logging town and now a ghost town, that derives from an Indian word meaning "where the wind blows from all directions." In fact, SR 112 to Port Angeles can be exceedingly windy.

No longer inland, the drive near **Clallam Bay** provides picture-pretty views of the strait. **Sekiu** is a tiny waterfront community well known for recreational fishing and scuba diving. Even small fishing boats can access these fishing grounds.

Do stop at **Neah Bay,** the reservation of the Makah Nation. The **Makah Nations Museum** displays baskets, replicas of canoes, and photographs but is probably best known for its accurate model of Makah lodging, based on findings from a Washington State University archaeological dig near Lake Ozette, near the coast, in the early '80s. During that time archaeologists painstakingly analyzed a preserved village that a tidal erosion uncovered. One of the other fascinating aspects of the excavation is that the diggers didn't use picks or shovels, only sea water to remove debris from the remains, which had been covered by a mudslide 500 years earlier.

Now travel southeast on SR 112 until it intersects with SR 113. When you arrive in **Sappho,** head southwest on US 101 to enter the **Olympic National Park.**

If you aren't too hungry, take a detour west on SR 110 to **La Push,** on Washington's northernmost coast in the Quileute Indian village. First Beach is considered the most pristine beach in the Northwest. Gigantic rocks tower over the mile-wide, crescent-shaped shoreline.

The town of **Forks** is right on US 101. During the summer, the highway can become a congested thoroughfare, especially with families whose children are enamored with the "Twilight" book series by Stephenie Meyer, who lives in Arizona but whose characters live in Forks, Washington. The town offers tours of the spots around town where the characters play out their lives, such as Forks High School and the parking lot where a *Twilight* character is rescued.

Chinook Pharmacy, 11 S. Forks Ave. (360-374-2294), is a good place to stop for sundries and a few souvenir items. They also have a nice selection of Northwest travel books. Fern Gallery, next door, is a coffee/antiques/souvenir shop that sells inexpensive Native earrings and dream-catchers. **JT's Sweet Stuffs,** 80 N. Forks Ave. (360-374-6111), an ice cream and candy shop, is on the opposite side of the street.

LUNCH   **Forks Coffee Shop,** 241 S. Forks Ave.; (360) 374-6769. Don't let the raw appearance send you in another direction. The cafe is clean inside and offers standard, well-prepared American food in large quantities for breakfast, lunch, and dinner.

AFTERNOON

Your lake lodge and more than 250 miles of hiking trails are waiting for you in the Quinalt Valley, but don't overlook **Ruby Beach,** south of Forks, even for a short stop. It's a photo-perfect opportunity: Monolithic rocks hover over the deserted beach, which is strewn with oddly shaped pieces of driftwood.

DINNER **Roosevelt Dining Room,** named after President Franklin D. Roosevelt, who dined in the lodge in 1937. The prices are on the high end, but your meal there, and the views of the lake, will linger in your memory for a long time. Very good beef, fish, and pasta entrees.

LODGING **Lake Quinalt Lodge,** 345 South Shore Rd.; (800) 562-6672 . Built in 1926, the caretakers have furnished many main lodge rooms with antiques. Eight boathouse rooms are suitable for families with pets. There's an indoor pool, a sauna, and game rooms. The lodge was presented as one of the "great lodges of national parks" on PBS. In the summer, deep blue hydrangeas and pink foxglove are prolific, even next to the busy forest service road that gives entry to the forest. Just down the road from the lodge are a post office, a mercantile, cafe, gas station, and forest service office.

MORNING / DAY 2

BREAKFAST You'll start your day with healthy fare such as homemade granola and fruit, or steel-cut oatmeal, or perhaps with heartier entrees that include sweet potato pancakes or brioche French toast.

Get an early start to allow time for a short hike through temperate rain forest. The Maple Glad Rain Forest Trail begins across the bridge from the Quinalt Ranger Station, just down the road from the lodge.

A walk along this ½-mile trail takes about 30 minutes. Naturally, big leaf maples are everywhere, engulfed by moss and ferns. The 1-mile Graves Creek Nature trailhead begins at Graves Creek campground, along the shore of the Quinault River, about 16 miles east on South Shore Road. For other hiking choices, see **Olympic National Park service maps,** www.nps.gov/olym/planyourvisit/maps.htm.

You can return home the way you arrived, or drive back on US 101 south, southeast on SR 12, and SR 8 to Olympia and I-5.

There's More . . . .

Hiking. **Sol Duc Falls,** 26 miles east of Forks. Trail guides available at trailhead. Wide gravel trail and a railed viewing area at the falls.

Museums. **Forks Timber Museum,** US 101, as you enter town from the south; (360) 374-9663; www.forks-web.com/fg/timbermuseum .htm. Highlights the region's homesteading and logging history, with displays dating back to the 1870s.

Special Events . . . .

AUGUST
Makah Days, Neah Bay. Three-day event with canoe races, a salmon bake, a talent show, dancing, and fireworks.

LATE SEPTEMBER–EARLY OCTOBER
Last Chance Salmon Derby, La Push. The event celebrates the last opportunity in the season to fish for salmon, and those who enter the salmon derby are eligible for cash prizes if they succeed in reeling one in. Coincides with the community's fish and brew dinner. Features music and dancing.

Other Restaurants and Lodging . . . .

AMANDA PARK

Lake Quinalt Resort, 314 N. Shore Rd.; (360) 288-2362 or (800) 650-2362; www.lakequinault.com. Recently remodeled rooms, including townhouse suites that sleep up to 6 and kitchenette units. Parklike setting with a deck, gazebo, and lake views.

Quinalt River Inn, 8 River Dr.; (360) 288-2237 or (800) 410-2237; www.quinaultriverinn.com. Accommodations are well-cared-for, grounds nicely maintained. Refrigerators, satellite TV in rooms. A general store and 2 cafes within easy walking distance.

CLALLAM BAY

Winter Summer Inn B&B, 16651 SR 112; (360) 963-2264; www .wintersummerinn.com. Late 1800s home located between the Strait of Juan de Fuca and the Olympic Mountains. Beautiful views from the deck of the strait, Vancouver Island, and beautiful sunsets. One suite with a fully equipped kitchen and 3 rooms. Includes a full breakfast, sometimes with homemade Danish or cinnamon rolls.

FORKS

Kalaloch Lodge, 157151 US 101; (866) 525-2562; www.olympic nationalparks.com/accommodations/kalaloch-lodge.aspx. Built in 1953; offers basic accommodations in 2 ocean-view suites, 3 ocean-view rooms, and several cabins. The crowning glory of this facility is the beach, just steps away.

Miller Tree Inn Bed & Breakfast, 654 E. Division St.; (360) 374-6806 or (800) 943-6563; www.millertreeinn.com. Casual, welcoming atmosphere in a 1916 farmhouse. Five rooms, 2 suites, and a 1-bedroom apartment. Country furnishings and modern amenities. Guests sit on porch and drink iced tea and lemonade.

Pacific Inn Motel, 352 Forks Ave.; (800) 235-7344; www.pacific innmotel.com. Located in downtown Forks, these clean and simple rooms are reasonably priced, and include microwaves, refrigerators, and wireless Internet. On-site laundry is a convenience that visiting families appreciate.

SEKIU
Van Riper's Resort, 280 Front St.; (360) 963-2334 or (888) 462-0803; www.vanripersresort.com/aboutresort.htm. Motel with 16 one-bed rooms and suites, right on the waterfront.

For More Information . . . .

Forks Chamber of Commerce, 1411 S. Forks Ave., P.O. Box 1249, Forks, WA 98331; (360) 374-2531; www.forkswa.com.

Neah Bay Chamber of Commerce, 1081 Bayview Ave., P.O. Box 249, Neah Bay, WA 98357; (360) 645-2711; www.neahbaywa .com.

Olympic National Park, 600 E. Park Ave., Port Angeles, WA 98362; (360) 565-3130; www.nps.gov/olym.

Olympic National Park service maps, www.nps.gov/olym/planyour visit/maps.htm

Olympic Peninsula Visitor Bureau, 338 W. 1st St., Suite 104, Port Angeles, WA 98362; (800) 942-4042 or (360) 457-8527; www .olympicpeninsula.org.

INDEX

Tumwater Canyon, 106
Turtleback Farm Inn, 17
Twede's Cafe, 86
Twilight, 216
Twisp, 97
Twisp Chamber of
    Commerce, 102
Two-day Ethnic Fest, 184
Two River Heritage
    Museum, 146

U

UBC Museum of Anthropology
    Museum Shop, 34
Uncommon Gift, The, 145
University of British Columbia
    Museum of Anthropology, 33

V

Valley Cafe, 111
Vancouver Aquarium Marine
    Science Center, 35
Vancouver Art Gallery, 36
Vancouver Boat Tours, 36
Vancouver, British
    Columbia, 30
Vancouver Farmers
    Market, 144
Vancouver Folk Music
    Festival, 37
Vancouver, George, 192

Vancouver International Film
    Festival, 38
Vancouver International Jazz
    Festival, 38
Vancouver Public Library, 33
Van Riper's Resort, 220
Verksted Gallery, 191
Verlot Ranger Station, 91
Victoria, B.C., 202
Viking Fest, 196
Viking Hall, 10
Vinny's Ristorante, 21
Visconti's, 107

W

Wade Gallery, 135
Waikiki Beach, 128
Wallace Falls State Park, 105
Waring, Guy, 96
Warms Springs Inn Bed and
    Breakfast, 120
Washington and British
    Columbia Border
    Information, 41
Washington Apple Commission
    Visitor Center, 109
Washington Pass Overlook, 95
Washington State Apple
    Blossom Festival, 114
Washington State Ferries, 29,
    63, 212